# Do Thyself No Harm

## Recovering Lost Hope

By

Rick Carter Jr Ph.D.

*Do Thyself No Harm*

*Recovering Lost Hope*

Rick Carter Jr. Ph.D.

Writings contained herein are by the author unless otherwise stated.

All scriptures are taken from the King James Bible.

Copyright © 2021
All rights reserved.

ISBN: 9798712703012

IBA Publishing
2424 SW 135th St
Oklahoma City, OK 73170

www.hope4addictions.com
www.ibadirect.com

# CONTENTS

| | |
|---|---|
| Let's Ask Why | Pg 1 |
| The Right Perspective of Spiritual Warfare | Pg 5 |
| A Preliminary Weapon | Pg 11 |
| Understanding Your Position in Christ | Pg 17 |
| Accepting Your New Identity in Christ | Pg 21 |
| Finding Your Purpose in Christ | Pg 29 |
| Growing Boldness and Confidence | Pg 33 |
| The Nature of the Fight | Pg 37 |
| The Structure of the Enemy | Pg 43 |
| The Strength of the Enemy | Pg 49 |
| The Scope of the Enemy | Pg 57 |
| The Subtlety of the Enemy | Pg 63 |
| Developing Tactical Awareness: Identifying the Access Points | Pg 71 |
| Closing the Access | Pg 77 |
| Maintaining Your Security | Pg 81 |
| Loss Control or Insecurity Issues | Pg 83 |
| Lack of or Loss of Identity | Pg 93 |
| Loss of a Sense of Purpose | Pg 119 |
| Feeling Despised or Shamed | Pg 125 |
| Overcome with Guilt | Pg 135 |
| Feelings of Failure or Blinded by the Darkness | Pg 143 |
| Prolonged Sickness and Trials | Pg 149 |
| Being Threatened or Bullied | Pg 155 |
| Depression | Pg 161 |
| Bitterness | Pg 173 |

One

# *Let's Ask Why*

Hope: A desire of some good, accompanied with at least a slight expectation of obtaining it, or a belief that it is obtainable. – Webster's 1828 Dictionary, Definition 1

Suicide, by many accounts, has reached the level of an epidemic not only in the U.S., but worldwide. It is estimated that in 2017, suicide was the 10th leading cause of death in the U.S., but among people ages 10-34, it was the second leading cause. This gets even worse when you realize that only one in twenty-five suicide attempts is successful. The specific reasons for suicide vary widely based upon each individual. Some reasons given include guilt, shame, bullying, a sense of worthlessness, depression, addiction, inability to deal with trauma, grief, or inability to deal with a loss of ability, power, wealth, or identity. Whatever the individual reason is they all have one thing in common. The individual has reached a point where they have lost hope that things can get better, hope that there is a purpose or hope that what is better can be obtained by them. Maybe you know someone who has attempted or committed suicide, or maybe you are considering it yourself. I write today to give you hope.

You may doubt that this hope is possible, but I have confidence that it is available to you. For a few minutes, I ask you to borrow my confidence, if you lack your own. I am convinced that a serious mistake has been made in our world. To rid ourselves of what might be considered by some as oppression, we have inadvertently also gotten rid of that which provides hope. You see, some years ago Western society set out to rid themselves of God. They championed the idea that there was no God and that those who believed in God were superstitious and weak. Every person was supposed to stand on their own and would not answer to some oppressive God who would judge them. Now people are supposed to be free of all that restriction and in their freedom, they can pursue their version of pleasure.

The problem is that in casting off God, we have also cast off any purpose to life. If there is no God, then there is no purpose for life. We are just a cosmic accident and there is no ultimate reason to live. Those men were wrong! I will not go into the specifics here, but there is significant reason to believe that there is a God and that He has a purpose for your life. I submit to you my testimony of belief and the testimony of multitudes of others who have found hope and purpose in God. In like manner, I want to introduce you to the reality that God's Word, the Bible, has explored and expressed much on this issue of suicide. Before you dismiss this, take a minute and consider that the Bible shows us seven men who committed suicide, one that intended to commit suicide, and several more that wished they would die. In all of these instances, we find reasons that people lose hope and consider suicide. The interesting thing about the Bible is that it not only addresses the reasons people lose hope and attempt suicide, but it also gives us an answer to these issues and shows how hope can be restored.

I imagine that many people who read this will be surprised at the details of the people that considered or committed suicide in the Bible and the fact that the descriptions in the Bible provide so much insight into why they did so. The Bible is full of understanding and help in every area of life. The greatest news is that the Bible also gives us an answer concerning how to find hope again. Maybe one of these areas will mirror your circumstances or maybe you are reading this book to find help for someone else, either way, the answers here are not new ideas, they have been tested in time and found to be true.

Hebrews 6:17-19 tells us about a place where we can find hope, and not just any hope but the kind of hope that can be an anchor for our souls. A place where we can be secure and have a refuge from the problems that we are facing. It says, "Wherein God, willing more abundantly to shew unto the heirs of promise the immutability of his counsel, confirmed it by an oath: That by two immutable things, in which it was impossible for God to lie, we might have a strong consolation, who have fled for refuge to lay hold upon the hope set before us: Which hope we have as an anchor of the soul, both sure and stedfast, and which entereth into that within the veil;"

Let's consider this hope that the Bible speaks of for a moment before looking at specific problems we face. The hope spoken of in the Bible is not a place to go to as much as a person who came for you. That person is Jesus Christ. He is the hope that the Bible is talking about and it is in Him that you can find new and secure hope and life. In the thieves of hope, you will see examples of the reasons for suicide that are in the Bible, but Jesus said in John 10:10 "The thief cometh not, but for to steal, and to kill, and to destroy: I am come that they might have life, and that they might have it more abundantly." You see, Jesus came to give you a new life, one that is filled with abundance, one that is filled with peace. He provided this new life for us by taking our place in death. He allowed Himself to be killed for our sin and died in our place. It says in Romans 5:8 "But God commendeth his love toward us, in that, while we were yet sinners, Christ died for us." Jesus Christ died for you so that you won't have to. The life that you are weary of right now He already died for and is offering you a new life in its place. Jesus said in John 3:16-18, "For God so loved the world, that he gave his only begotten Son, that whosoever believeth in him should not perish, but have everlasting life. For God sent not his Son into the world to condemn the world; but that the world through him might be saved. He that believeth on him is not condemned: but he that believeth not is condemned already, because he hath not believed in the name of the only begotten Son of God." This is actually the message of the Bible, that God, in love, sent Jesus to take our sin upon Himself and die in our place so that we can have a new life in Him. If you are tired of the life you have now, don't end it by suicide, instead, exchange it for a new life in Christ. Receive Him as your Savior and He will give you the life that you have been missing.

Apart from Jesus, there is only death and sorrow but in Christ, there is life and peace. That is the hope that God offers you through Jesus Christ, strong confidence that your sins have been covered no matter what they are, and peace with God because you have been redeemed by Him from all your troubles. He offers you a new hope, a new life, and with it a new identity. In 2 Corinthians 5:17 the Bible tells us, "Therefore if any man be in Christ, he is a new creature: old things are passed away; behold, all things are become new." This new identity means that you can put the past behind you and start over with a clean slate. God wants you to have the freedom to experience the life He intended you to have in Christ. I encourage you to stop right now and call on Jesus Christ to be your Savior, confess your sin to Him and ask Him for forgiveness. That is why He died for you. Claim your new life and a new identity in Christ and grab hold of the hope that is set before you.

Hope: "Confidence in a future event; the highest degree of well-founded expectation of good; as a hope founded on God's gracious promises; a scriptural sense." – Webster's 1828 Dictionary, Definition 2

Romans 10:8-13 "But what saith it? The word is nigh thee, even in thy mouth, and in thy heart: that is, the word of faith, which we preach; That if thou shalt confess with thy mouth the Lord Jesus, and shalt believe in thine heart that God hath raised him from the dead, thou shalt be saved. For with the heart man believeth unto righteousness; and with the mouth confession is made unto salvation. For the scripture saith, Whosoever believeth on him shall not be ashamed. For there is no difference between the Jew and the Greek: for the same Lord over all is rich unto all that call upon him. For whosoever shall call upon the name of the Lord shall be saved."

Titus 3:7 "That being justified by his grace, we should be made heirs according to the hope of eternal life."

Two

# *The Right Perspective of Spiritual Warfare*

I have yet to encounter a situation where a person was suicidal, that they weren't also facing a significant spiritual attack against them. Just as sure as there is a God, there is also a Devil. He hates God and everything that God loves. There is ample evidence as you will see that we as humans can be affected by demonic work. I am not saying that any person who considers suicide was made to by the Devil. The Devil cannot make you do anything. Demons can however speak to us in a way to encourage sinful and destructive thoughts. Many of the suicidal thoughts that people have are not actually their own, they are hearing actually the voices of those who wish them harm speaking as if they were. If you are going to gain victory over the thoughts of suicide, you must begin by shutting up the demonic voices that are cheering for it to happen. The first several chapters here are designed to help you do that. The last portion of this book is to deal with the specific issues stole hope and gave rise to their influence. I pray that you take your time in the first part of this book to thoroughly close the access that has been given to demonic influence so that there can be victory over the underlying issues.

Over my years of ministry, I have seen two dramatically different approaches to the topic of spiritual warfare. On one hand, you have those who totally ignore it and act as if there is no such thing as demonic activity. These people tend to be willfully ignorant of Satan's influence and blame it all simply on man's sinful will. To be sure, a great number of our troubles are directly linked to our own sinful choices. However, to ignore the clear teaching from God's Word on the reality of demonic influence is not wise. On the other side of the issue are those who see a demon behind every whistling tea pot. In their view, every problem is a demonic problem. This reminds me of the third law of theology, for every theological position there is an equal and opposite position (sarcasm). I have yet to find the topic in which the extreme position is the right one. The Bible is very clear that the Devil is a real person who actively works in the affairs of men to seduce them into rebellion against God, and yet, that men in fact do also have a sinful nature that itself entices them to sinful endeavor and bondage is beyond question. Both of these things are true at the same time, and the answer to dealing with them is not to point the finger of blame exclusively at the Devil but it is also not to ignore him.

Often however, because of this divergence of ideas, those who deal with spiritual warfare do so with a gasping breath at the power of the Devil. Many Christians are filled with fear concerning the Devil and his work. Might I remind you though, that God has not given us a spirit of fear, but of power and of love and of a sound mind. Teaching on spiritual warfare that leaves a person with a fear of the Devil has been overly focused on the Devil and ignores the reality that God has already won the war. The cross forever settled the question of victory in the life of those who are saved and truly, greater is He that is within us than he that is in the world. In this we should rejoice, not cower in fear.

The four gospels are given to provide us a fourfold view of Jesus Christ. In Matthew, we see Him as the King. In Mark, we see Him as the servant. In Luke, we see Him as the Son of Man, and then in John we see Him as the Son of God. What a wonderful blessing it is to see Jesus from all of these views and gain a deeper and more profound understanding of who He is. In a similar manner, God has also given us four views of the believer in the books of Galatians, Ephesians, Philippians, and Colossians. In each of these books we see how the attributes of Christ in us relate to living out the Christian faith. In Galatians, we see how a Christian should relate to those around them, the outer man. In Ephesians, we see how a Christian should relate to the attacks of Satan, the spiritual man. In Philippians, we see how a Christian should relate to their own inward struggles, the inner man. In Colossians, we see how a Christian should relate to Christ, the perfect man. In each of these books the same attributes of the believer are expressed in a slightly different way to show how they aid us in growing closer to God and to the image of Christ.

The book of Ephesians then should be examined to understand how a believer is to deal with spiritual warfare. When we look at Ephesians, we see though that the Devil is not even mentioned until the very end of the book. That is because it is far more important to focus on God, who He is, and what He is doing in us. Now, when we consider this truth and the illustration from the Bible of dealing with the attacks of the Devil, we find that God uses the illustration of warfare to explain it. He tells us that we are to put on "The armor of God", and He calls the Devil our adversary and enemy. Thus, the imagery of the believer as a soldier is very clear in the Bible. For a minute let us consider what we know about soldiers and make some obvious applications to our own experience in this spiritual battle.

When a soldier enters the military, they go through a process designed to prepare them for battle. That process has several important factors that will be relevant to our study on spiritual warfare. First, the candidate will process into the military, including a swearing in ceremony. A new believer has in a sense sworn into the Lord's Army when they accept Christ as their Savior. There is a commitment made on their part but on God's part things are even more secure than the military. The Bible tells us that God seals us with the Holy Spirit (2 Corinthians 1:22, Ephesians 1:13, Ephesians 4:30) and keeps us by His power (1 Peter 1:5).

Once they have processed into the military, the candidate then goes to boot camp. Here at boot camp they will receive a new look, a new schedule and a new identity. Their new look includes a haircut and a uniform. While the outer appearance is not the first thing that God works on in a believer, we know that the outer man will certainly begin to reflect what is on the inside and a believer will put away worldly appearances and identification from the flesh if they are walking with the Lord.

The new schedule that a soldier takes on is one that has been designed to make them stronger. They have a new time to get up and go to bed, they have times of physical exercise and drill, as well as times of study and instruction. They must learn to march and even walk correctly. There will be obstacle courses that they must master and physical challenges that they must overcome. Similarly, the new believer will have direction for a new schedule from our commander. We have been told not to forsake assembling together in the church house (Hebrews 10:25). We have been instructed to walk with God personally, which means that daily we should be setting aside time to read God's Word and pray. Having a daily devotional time with God will, at length, determine the success that you have as a soldier of the cross. We have also been called to serve the Lord which will mean being involved in outreach and soul winning that we will need to make a designated part of our schedule if it is to be accomplished. As we begin keeping this new schedule, there will be tests and obstacles that we will have to overcome to be faithful to the Lord and grow.

A new identity is drilled into the soldier in many ways, from the uniform to the activities, but much of it is accomplished by immersing the soldier in the culture of the military. The candidate is taken from being a civilian to being a soldier; their identity changes, their mindset changes and their commitment grows. They will be taught that the way they used to do things is not how they will be doing them in the future. They will be taught about the history and purpose of the branch of the service they represent. They will be taught how to recognize an imposter and keep them from entering the protected area. I am told that many people wash out of boot camp at this stage, either because they fail to conform, perform or to pass the tests regarding the branch of service and their responsibilities. The soldier is not taught alone but as part of a unit and in that unit there is a strong emphasis on unity. They are taught the need to support and help one another. They are taught the importance of marching in unison. No military could succeed if every member was off doing their own thing in their own way. The strength of the military is their unity and familiarity with the structure and order. Likewise the Lord's army is organized into units through local New Testament Churches. Each church may function slightly different from another, but they all have the same commander and directive. For the new believer, it is important to learn the new position that they have in Christ. They are no longer in their sin but now are in Christ and along with our new position comes a great benefit of belonging and promise. The new believer must also learn to appropriate their new identity because of their position in Christ. They are not what they were, they are a new creation (2 Corinthians 5:17, Galatians 6:15).

Before the soldier moves on to their active duty station, they will also be assigned a purpose in the service. Based upon his aptitude and testing, he will generally have some choices to make about what job they will get to do. From there they will set out to their purpose in the service. Similarly, God has a purpose for each believer. His will is shown to us by His Word, the leadership of the Holy Ghost and the counsel of those pastors and teachers He has put over us in the church.

Much like the military, God wants to take us once we are saved and give us a new position in Christ, a new identity and a new purpose. Once we have these things down, we can move on to some more specific training in how to combat our enemy. Did you notice how much training goes into preparing a soldier before they ever deal with a specific enemy? They don't give them specifics about an enemy in boot camp because they are not yet facing a specific enemy. The enemy they fight in boot camp is their own physical and mental disciplines. Once they are out of boot camp, they will be taught more specifics about the enemy as needed. First though, they must learn to eliminate their own vulnerabilities. They must learn tactical awareness and self-defense skills that will protect them from any enemy that they will face. Some of this is done in boot camp and some will be done with extended or specialized and continual training that they will engage in.

Likewise, God wants us to gain tactical awareness in our Christian life. In a sense the greatest danger isn't the enemy, it is the access we give to him. There is a specific way that the base is to be defended, there are specific check points and a secure perimeter that is established. No one is allowed on the base without proper verification that they should be there. This is often one of the greatest problems that a believer faces. They have allowed access to the enemy because they have not closed off the access points in their lives.

The purpose of this study is to walk you through the processes that are found in the book of Ephesians. If you follow this pattern you will be a good soldier of Jesus Christ and you will be fit for the battle. I want to encourage you to be diligent in your endeavor here and commit yourself to full honesty and willingness to deal with everything that God brings out to you in this process. If you do, you will find victory over the enemy is available to every soldier in the Lord's army.

# Three

# *A Preliminary Weapon*

Revelation 12:7-11 "And there was war in heaven: Michael and his angels fought against the dragon; and the dragon fought and his angels, And prevailed not; neither was their place found any more in heaven. And the great dragon was cast out, that old serpent, called the Devil, and Satan, which deceiveth the whole world: he was cast out into the earth, and his angels were cast out with him. And I heard a loud voice saying in heaven, Now is come salvation, and strength, and the kingdom of our God, and the power of his Christ: for the accuser of our brethren is cast down, which accused them before our God day and night. And they overcame him by the blood of the Lamb, and by the word of their testimony; and they loved not their lives unto the death."

Satan is a liar but he is a very good one. He is also called here the accuser of the brethren. As you embark in this process of spiritual warfare you are going to need to keep your eyes on Christ. I want to start off here showing you that Satan is already a defeated foe. He has lost the war and thought he is more powerful than you and I, He is not more powerful than our God. 1 John 4:4 "Ye are of God, little children, and have overcome them: because greater is he that is in you, than he that is in the world." Though it might be a bit fearful to consider dealing with spiritual conflict there is nothing to fear, God has already won the war and we are just claiming His victory. Remember that God doesn't give us a spirit of fear, this comes from the lies of the devil. 2 Timothy 1:7 "For God hath not given us the spirit of fear; but of power, and of love, and of a sound mind."

As you work through this book it is likely that Satan will accuse you of your past to try and get you to stop claiming your present position and identity in Christ. When this happens, then it is time to practice the 3 P's found in this passage that overcome the devil and his accusations. The accusations that you are likely to encounter may be about your past. These accusations could be about sins that you have committed, conflicts you have had or things that you knew you should have done but didn't. Other accusations may be about the present, thoughts against other people especially your authorities or the idea that you should commit some sin. The accusations may also be about your future, that you won't ever be able to have victory or that you will fall again. The devil is a master at accusations and he knows what you are most vulnerable too, but God's Word is the answer and following it will give you victory over those accusations.

There are three steps outlined in Revelation 12:11 that you should follow to get victory over the accusations. First, Plead the Blood, it says that they overcame him (the devil) by the blood of the Lamb. Since you are saved your past sin has been placed under the blood of Jesus Christ and God has forgiven it. Regardless of what the devil says, God says it is forgiven, you must come to faith that the Bible is true regardless of what you think or how you feel. Look what the Bible says about this.

> Ephesians 1:7 "In whom we have redemption through his blood, the forgiveness of sins, according to the riches of his grace;"
>
> Colossians 1:14 "In whom we have redemption through his blood, even the forgiveness of sins:"
>
> Colossians 1:20 "And, having made peace through the blood of his cross, by him to reconcile all things unto himself; by him, I say, whether they be things in earth, or things in heaven."
>
> Hebrews 9:12 "Neither by the blood of goats and calves, but by his own blood he entered in once into the holy place, having obtained eternal redemption for us."

> 1 Peter 1:18-19 "Forasmuch as ye know that ye were not redeemed with corruptible things, as silver and gold, from your vain conversation received by tradition from your fathers; But with the precious blood of Christ, as of a lamb without blemish and without spot:"
>
> Romans 8:1 "There is therefore now no condemnation to them which are in Christ Jesus, who walk not after the flesh, but after the Spirit."
>
> John 3:18 "<u>He that believeth on him is not condemned</u>: but he that believeth not is condemned already, because he hath not believed in the name of the only begotten Son of God."

Do you see, the blood is the answer for sin, when the devil accuses us of sin then we plead the blood against his accusation. We are forgiven because of the blood and it is settled.

The next thing that you must do is Praise the Lord. Revelation 12:11 says they not only overcame by the blood of the Lamb but also by the word of their testimony. Our testimony is what God has done for us. Simply begin to praise the Lord out loud for all that He has done for you and then continue to praise Him for everything you can see or think of until the Devil withdraws from attacking you. It may take a few minutes of praising the Lord, it may take longer but do not stop until you know the peace of God.

We are told in James 4:7-8 "Submit yourselves therefore to God. Resist the devil, and he will flee from you. Draw nigh to God, and he will draw nigh to you. Cleanse your hands, ye sinners; and purify your hearts, ye double minded." The act of resisting the devil is found in the process of drawing neigh to God. If you want to resist the devil remember that he must submit to God. If you want to be closer to God your approach must be made by thanksgiving and praise. It tells us in Psalms 22:3 "But thou art holy, O thou that inhabitest the praises of Israel."

We know according to Isaiah 61:3 that God will lift a heavy spirit when we engage in praising Him. "To appoint unto them that mourn in Zion, to give unto them beauty for ashes, the oil of joy for mourning, the garment of praise for the spirit of heaviness; that they might be called trees of righteousness, the planting of the LORD, that he might be glorified." As a matter of fact, it tells us in Psalms 100:4 that thanksgiving and praise are the way that we can come into the very presence of God. "Enter into his gates with thanksgiving, and into his courts with praise: be thankful unto him, and bless his name."

So what is praise? It says in Hebrews 13:15 "By him therefore let us offer the sacrifice of praise to God continually, that is, the fruit of our lips giving thanks to his name." In the book of Psalms you often see David begin to thank God for what He has done and this turns into praise for who He is or His character. To thank God all you have to do is look around you, He created everything. Start thanking and praising Him for everything you see and you will begin to draw into His presence and as you do the devil will be forced to flee.

Now this doesn't mean he will stay gone. As a matter of fact, often as you start this process you will find that he will attack you even more. I don't say that to discourage you, I say it to prepare you. When you draw neigh to God it makes the devils scared, they have had dominance over you in this area and they don't want to lose it so they want to convince you that what you're doing won't work. Much like a bully will be even meaner when he is losing control. Don't be fooled, they cannot stand up against God and His Word. When they attack again simply follow the same plan again and again until they realize that you are serious and that you will not be detoured. Eventually they will leave you alone because you are doing the opposite of what they want. The last thing that they want is to drive you closer to God so they will look for some other area of attack. Don't worry, we are going to close off all their access as we go through this.

The final "P" is to Practice the truth. It says that they loved not their lives unto the death. This means to continue to do what you know God has called you to do. Be obedient to the truth, do what is right, don't turn away. As you continue to stand fast in the truth the devils must concede defeat.

Did you catch it, Plead the blood, Praise the Lord and Practice the truth. This is the recipe that is shown in the Bible to overcome the evil one. It works and it will work for you. As you work through this book keep this tool in mind and practice it when you hear the accuser. Victory awaits you.

# DO THYSELF NO HARM

Four

# *Understanding Your Position in Christ*

To understand your position in Christ, think of our analogy concerning a soldier. When someone joins the military, they are inducted into a specific branch of the service. Once they are in, their position is different than it was. They are no longer a civilian, they are now a soldier. This new position has unique responsibilities as well as specific privileges. The new position completely transforms their entire life as they begin to adapt to the new culture that they have joined. Culture is an important thing to understand. While a soldier interacts with the civilian culture that they are in, they in fact have a distinct culture that they are part of. They can be influenced of course by the civilian culture, but they are responsible to the military culture. A new way of thinking and acting is inherent in the new culture.

Just as there are things that are true for every soldier because of their position in the military, there are things that are true for every believer. Your position in Christ includes a completely new culture that you have been made a part of and to which you are called to adhere. To understand this culture, we are going to take a look at the first three chapters of Ephesians. Here we find a very important word that will help us identify the specifics about our position as a believer, the word "in". Your assignment to begin this section is to read through the first three chapters of Ephesians and compare it with the list on the following page about the believer's position in Christ. In other words, these things are true about us because we are believers in Christ. The word "in" will help you to identify what is true about our position. It may say, "in Christ", "in Him", "in Whom" or some other variation.

As you read this passage and compare it to the list below circle the number by any of these truths that you struggle to believe apply to you. Once you have finished take 3x5 cards and write any of the truths that you have circled on the cards. These are going to be your affirmation cards. You see these things are true even if you don't see them as true for yourself. You must come to faith on their application to your life. Each day read them out laud both the truth and the verse until you accept them as truth and know in your heart that they apply to you.

## Our Position in Christ according to Ephesians

In Christ, believers...
1. Are saints – 1:1
2. Are called faithful – 1:1
3. Have grace – 1:2
4. Have peace – 1:2
5. Are blessed with all spiritual blessings – 1:3
6. Are in heavenly places – 1:3
7. Are chosen – 1:4
8. Are holy – 1:4
9. Are without blame – 1:4
10. Are before Him in love – 1:4
11. Are predestined to the adoption of children – 1:5
12. Are made accepted in the beloved – 1:6
13. Have redemption – 1:7
14. Have forgiveness – 1:7
15. Have the wisdom, prudence and will of God made know to us – 1:8-9
16. Will be gathered together – 1:10
17. Have obtained an inheritance – 1:11
18. Are to the praise of His glory – 1:12
19. Are sealed with the Holy Spirit of promise – 1:13
20. Can receive the spirit of wisdom and revelation – 1:17
21. Can have our understanding enlightened – 1:18
22. Have been made alive – 2:5
23. Are raised up with Christ – 2:6
24. Are made to sit together in heavenly places – 2:6
25. Will be shown the exceeding riches of His grace in His kindness – 2:7
26. Are the workmanship of God – 2:10
27. Are created in Christ unto good works – 2:10
28. Are ordained by God to walk in good works – 2:10
29. Are made nigh by the blood of Christ – 2:13
30. Have been reconciled to God – 2:16
31. Have access by one Spirit unto the Father – 2:18
32. Are made citizens with the saints – 2:19

33. Are of the household of God – 2:19
34. Are built upon the foundation of the apostles and prophets – 2:20
35. Have Jesus Christ as their chief corner stone – 2:20
36. Are growing as a temple of God – 2:21
37. Are built together for a habitation of God through the Spirit – 2:22
38. Are made heirs – 3:6
39. Are made partakers of His promise – 3:6
40. Have received an eternal purpose – 3:11
41. Have boldness – 3:12
42. Have access with confidence by faith – 3:12
43. Have been made part of the family of God – 3:15
44. Can be strengthened with might by His Spirit in the inner man – 3:16
45. Have Christ dwelling in their hearts by faith – 3:17
46. Are able to comprehend the breadth, length, depth and height of the love of Christ – 3:18-19
47. May be filled with all the fulness of God – 3:19

Five

# *Accepting Your New Identity in Christ*

Now that you see the incredible position believers have been given because of being in Christ, it is time to make a more distinctly personal application. The position in Christ that believers are blessed with belongs to you. Everything that is true about any believer's position in Christ, according to the Bible, is also true about you. It doesn't matter if you don't feel that it's true; God's promises are not based upon your feelings. Our feelings have been developed by two factors, first, our past experiences and second, our thinking process.

Our past experiences have a way of molding us in dramatic ways. Those who have experienced traumatic events in their past will likely have a different view of themselves and their sense of personal worth than those who grew up in a more secure environment. Abuses, betrayals and conflicts mold us, sometimes in ways to protect ourselves from more hurt and sometimes in destructive ways. Many times substance abuse, self-harm and destructive living patterns are the result of trying to escape from or cope with past experiences. This is because experience has taught you that your position is vulnerable, and you are trying to find some place of refuge or peace. However, none of these things offered by the world to numb you to your past or alleviate the pain will actually work; at length they will simply bring more sorrow into your life.

The mind is unique and the level of trouble that we have had is directly related to our experiences. Someone who grows up in a home filled with alcohol and violence has a much higher threshold for it than someone who grows up in what we would consider a more stable home. Yet, those who grow up in those stable homes will many times interpret any stern statement or raised voice as a traumatic event. This is not to say that they don't experience trauma, but rather that your concept of trauma is directly tied to the amount of trauma that you have actually seen. It takes far less to traumatize someone who has grown up in a safer environment than someone who has grown up in a dangerous environment. Thus, a person who grows up in that safe environment can have as dramatic a reaction to what they perceive as trauma as anyone else.

It is not uncommon that people who grow up in homes of pastors and missionaries will fall into the same traps of addictions and destructive life choices as those who grow up in abusive or violent behavior. That is not to say that all pastor's and missionary's homes are indeed always safe from these things, but rather, that even if they are this does not preclude those who grow up in them from feeling a personal level of trauma based upon their own interpretation. In both of these situations, the reason is because of our thinking patterns.

Proverbs 23:7 "For as he thinketh in his heart, so is he: Eat and drink, saith he to thee; but his heart is not with thee."

Our experiences are interpreted by our thoughts. Sometimes they shape our thinking and sometimes our thinking shapes the experience. We have all probably had the experience of sharing a memory with family or friends only to have them try to correct our idea of what happened. Many times at family dinners or holidays, I have heard the phrase, "no, that's not how it happened". Yet our thinking patterns have interpreted what we experienced in a way unique to us. Two people can go through the same experience and come out the other side with very different views of what happened. The same experience can make some people angry and bitter and others grateful. Why would we turn out so differently? Because of how we thought about the event. If we thought "I cannot believe this happened to me, I don't deserve this", then we might get angry. If we thought "I cannot believe I made it through that without more problems, it could have been a lot worse", then we might be grateful.

Our thinking not only shapes what we believe about our past experiences, but it also shapes what we believe about our present realities. We will interpret current events based upon our thinking. That is why people can read the same report and come away with very different beliefs. That is why there are people who are very conservative and people who are very liberal. All the information in the middle is the same, but how we think about it determines how we interpret it.

Now let me bring this back to the topic at hand of spiritual warfare. Because of your past experiences and because of your thinking process, you have a certain view of yourself. That view may be based upon your past traumas or upon your sinful decisions. Either way, it is very different than the view God has of you. The problem is that many people get saved and struggle with accepting what God says about them. They still see themselves as lost and worldly sinners rather than redeemed forgiven children of God. They have a hard time reconciling what Jesus said in John 15:19 as being true of them. "If ye were of the world, the world would love his own: but because ye are not of the world, but I have chosen you out of the world, therefore the world hateth you." If you are saved, you are still physically in this world, but you are no longer of this world, meaning you have a new position in heavenly places. Along with this new position comes a new identity in Christ. God no longer sees you as a sinner, He now sees you as a saint. He no longer sees you as an enemy, He now sees you as a child and heir.

You see, everything that is true about a believer's position in Christ, is true about you! As a matter of fact, this is where your new identity comes from. It's not just that believers are forgiven, you are forgiven. It's not just that believers are accepted, you are accepted. The problem is that your past experiences and your thinking patterns may make it difficult to accept these truths as personally applicable to yourself. In such cases, it is necessary to recognize that God is always right. Romans 3:4 says, "God forbid: yea, let God be true, but every man a liar; as it is written, That thou mightest be justified in thy sayings, and mightest overcome when thou art judged." What you need to do is let God be true and count your past experiences and your thinking processes as things of the past; lies that the Devil would have you believe. You are, in fact, a new creation in Christ and as His new creation you have a different position and a different identity than you did before.

To help you establish this new identity in your mind, take the list of your position in Christ and re-write it to reflect what it says about your personal identity in Christ. This would look something like this.

Position: In Christ, believers…
1. Are saints – 1:1
2. Are called faithful – 1:1
3. Have grace – 1:2
4. Have peace – 1:2
5. Are blessed with all spiritual blessings – 1:3

Identity: In Christ, I…

1. am a saint
2. am called faithful
3. have grace
4. have peace
5. am blessed with all spiritual blessings.

Everything that is true about any believer in Christ is true about you if you are saved! Just as before take those truths about who you are that you struggle to accept and write them on the front side of a 3x5 card. On the back side write out the verse that relates to the truth. You might also look up more verses that reinforce this truth about you and write them out as well. The goal here is to change your thinking to God's thinking. Accept the Word of God as true when it goes against your past experiences and thinking processes and come to faith on the topic.

Coming to faith means that you reject what you used to believe and accept what God says is true. Since according to Romans 10:17 "So then faith cometh by hearing, and hearing by the word of God." The best way to come to faith on something you have trouble accepting is to saturate your mind with God's Word. Repent of the old lies and accept the truth of God. Once you have accepted the truth about what God says concerning your identity, then you can move on to the next one you struggle with. This process may take weeks or much longer. Don't wait until you have all of them established to move on to the next section. Simply do the assignment fully and once your cards are prepared, begin working on them one by one as you go on to the next section.

# DO THYSELF NO HARM

## Our Identity in Christ according to Ephesians

In Christ, I…

1. Am a saint – 1:1
2. Am called faithful – 1:1
3. Have grace – 1:2
4. Have peace – 1:2
5. Am blessed with all spiritual blessings – 1:3
6. Am in heavenly places – 1:3
7. Am chosen – 1:4
8. Am holy – 1:4
9. Am without blame – 1:4
10. Am before Him in love – 1:4
11. Am predestined to the adoption of children – 1:5
12. Am made accepted in the beloved – 1:6
13. Have redemption – 1:7
14. Have forgiveness – 1:7
15. Have the wisdom, prudence and will of God made known to me – 1:8-9
16. Will be gathered together – 1:10
17. Have obtained an inheritance – 1:11
18. Am to the praise of His glory – 1:12
19. Am sealed with the Holy Spirit of promise – 1:13
20. Can receive the spirit of wisdom and revelation – 1:17
21. Can have my understanding enlightened – 1:18
22. Have been made alive – 2:5
23. Am raised up with Christ – 2:6
24. Am made to sit together in heavenly places – 2:6
25. Will be shown the exceeding riches of His grace in His kindness – 2:7
26. Am the workmanship of God – 2:10
27. Am created in Christ unto good works – 2:10
28. Am ordained by God to walk in good works – 2:10
29. Am made nigh by the blood of Christ – 2:13
30. Have been reconciled to God – 2:16
31. Have access by one Spirit unto the Father – 2:18

32. Am made a citizen with the saints – 2:19
33. Am made part of the household of God – 2:19
34. Am built upon the foundation of the apostles and prophets – 2:20
35. Have Jesus Christ as my chief corner stone – 2:20
36. Am growing as a temple of God – 2:21
37. Am built together for a habitation of God through the Spirit – 2:22
38. Am made an heir – 3:6
39. Am made a partaker of His promise – 3:6
40. Have received an eternal purpose – 3:11
41. Have boldness – 3:12
42. Have access with confidence by faith – 3:12
43. Have been made part of the family of God – 3:15
44. Can be strengthened with might by His Spirit in the inner man – 3:16
45. Have Christ dwelling in my heart by faith – 3:17
46. Am able to comprehend the breadth, length, depth and height of the love of Christ – 3:18-19
47. May be filled with all the fulness of God – 3:19

# Six

# *Finding Your Purpose in Christ*

Once a soldier has finished boot camp and has a better understanding of their position and identity in the military, they move on to special training regarding their purpose. Purpose is a very important thing. It helps us keep focused. It helps us know what we need to learn and of course what we need to do. Every believer has a purpose given to them from God. Of course, sometimes our purposes will overlap. As in the military, keeping yourself in shape, continuing your education and training are part of the purpose that each soldier has; it is the same for the believer. We are all called to keep ourselves in spiritual shape and grow in the knowledge of God. The way that we do this is through daily devotional time with God. Spending time in God's Word and in prayer is vital if you are to keep yourself in spiritual fighting shape. Overall this helps to serve our greatest purpose. This purpose is discussed in the same chapters we have been studying in Ephesians.

> Ephesians 1:9 "Having made known unto us the mystery of his will, according to his good pleasure which he hath purposed in himself:"

> Ephesians 1:11 "In whom also we have obtained an inheritance, being predestinated according to the purpose of him who worketh all things after the counsel of his own will:"

> Ephesians 3:11 "According to the eternal purpose

<u>which he purposed in Christ Jesus our Lord:"</u>

Based upon the Scripture, it is clear to see that God's purpose for us was established in Jesus Christ. Meaning that the purpose God has for your life is found in your relationship to Him through Jesus Christ. If God's purpose is found in Christ, and you are in Christ, then God has a purpose for you. First of all, it was God's purpose for you to be saved through Christ but is also clear that God's purpose for you didn't end there. God's purpose for you also includes an inheritance and knowing His will. God's will is knowable. You can know both His general will (God's will for every person), and His specific will (God's will for you personally). Part of God's purpose for your life is to seek out and know His will, it clearly says so in Ephesians 1:9.

You can read more about knowing the will of God in my book *"Knowing God's Will"*. Here, however, we are going to focus on getting a big picture view of God's will that is true for every believer including you. To do that I want you to read these first three chapters of Ephesians again and pick out a verse there that seems to summarize what God's will is for us. The verse that summarizes this to me is…

> Ephesians 2:10 "For we are his workmanship, created in Christ Jesus unto good works, which God hath before ordained that we should walk in them."

What does it mean? God's purpose for every believer is to change us into the image of Christ so that our works reflect His works. God wants you to grow in Christ so much that your old nature is put off and Christ's nature is put on in its place. God wants you to grow in Christ so much that when people look at you, they see Christ.

## DO THYSELF NO HARM

Write your verse here:

_____

_____

_____

_____

# DO THYSELF NO HARM

# Seven

# *Growing Boldness and Confidence*

Ephesians 3:12 "In whom we have boldness and access with confidence by the faith of him."

To be effective, a soldier must have confidence and be bold. God wants that same thing from His children. He does not want us to walk in a fearful and timid manner. The devil takes advantage of us when we are either over-confident in the flesh or lack confidence in the Lord. Having a firm understanding of our position in Christ and our spiritual identity in Christ, as well as our purpose given from God, will stir in us a boldness and confidence to fight the spiritual battles in the power of Christ. It is not our power, but His power in us, that gives us confidence to move forward spiritually. We know that Christ has already won the war, He has already defeated the Devil, so our battle is not to gain victory, but rather to live in the victory that He has won.

> Romans 8:37 "Nay, in all these things we are more than conquerors through him that loved us."
>
> John 16:33 "These things I have spoken unto you, that in me ye might have peace. In the world ye shall have tribulation: but be of good cheer; I have overcome the world."
>
> 1 John 2:13 "I write unto you, fathers, because ye have known him that is from the beginning. I write

unto you, young men, because ye have overcome the wicked one. I write unto you, little children, because ye have known the Father."

1 John 2:14 "I have written unto you, fathers, because ye have known him that is from the beginning. I have written unto you, young men, because ye are strong, and the word of God abideth in you, and ye have overcome the wicked one."

1 John 4:4 "Ye are of God, little children, and have overcome them: because greater is he that is in you, than he that is in the world."

1 John 5:4 "For whatsoever is born of God overcometh the world: and this is the victory that overcometh the world, even our faith."

1 John 5:5 "Who is he that overcometh the world, but he that believeth that Jesus is the Son of God?"

1 Corinthians 15:57 "But thanks be to God, which giveth us the victory through our Lord Jesus Christ."

We have received the victory because we are in Christ and He defeated the Devil when He rose from the grave. Because of our position in Christ, we have that victory and He has given us a new identity rather than the old sinful one that we had. All of these things are true for you and it is why you can have boldness to engage in fighting the spiritual battles that you face and why you can have confidence as you go before the throne of God in prayer during those times. You are not a stranger to God, you are not on the outside looking in, you are in, you are seated with Christ, you are an heir of God and the sooner you accept this truth the sooner you will start to know the victory that Christ has already won for you.

The next five chapters also appear in *The Armor Plated Life volume 1*. I have included them here because it is now that we are going to learn more about our enemy. God has revealed everything we need to know and having this knowledge we are confident of His power and control over the issues of our lives.

# DO THYSELF NO HARM

Eight

# *The Nature of the Fight*

> Ephesians 6:12 "For we wrestle not against flesh and blood, but against principalities, against powers, against the rulers of the darkness of this world, against spiritual wickedness in high *places*."

Someone once noted the similarity between principles found in the Old Testament book of Joshua to those found in the book of Ephesians and has said that the book of Joshua is to the Old Testament what the book of Ephesians is to the New. In the book of Joshua, you find the children of Israel finally crossing over the Jordan River and entering into the Promised Land. The Promised Land is not a heaven; rather it pictures the victorious Christian life. There are battles to be fought there, and there are enemies that lurk, lying in wait for us to stumble and fall. The first three enemies in the Book of Joshua show us a picture of the three enemies that the believer faces.

First, when they came across the Jordan River, they faced the city of Jericho. Jericho represents the world. We are not to engage it, we are to walk around it and God will cast it down by His power and might. We are not to take anything from it as it will pollute us. As we saw in the case of Achan, it will bring destruction into our lives and families.

The second enemy that they faced in Canaan land was the city of Ai. Ai was a little city, and they thought they didn't even need God to defeat this foe. They set out to do it on their own, only to be defeated and brought to their face before God, seeking His help. Ai is a picture of the flesh: it is little, but it will rise up and defeat us time after time because we depend upon our own power and not upon the Lord.

The third enemy that is found in Joshua is the Gibeonites. These men came to Joshua and the children of Israel dressed in their oldest clothes, carrying moldy bread and empty bottles, as if they were from some great distance. They deceived Joshua and the men of Israel into making a truce with them, when the truth is that they were just from over the next hill. This enemy is subtle and filled with lies, and will come to you in whatever form and fashion that they need to in order to gain your trust and deceive you. They represent the devil. So in these three enemies, we see a picture of all the enemies of the believer: the world, the flesh, and the devil.

We are going to examine the first part of this verse with some depth and consider the nature of the battle against these enemies that we face in our Christian life. Now you notice that this verse begins with the word "for", meaning "because of something that was previously stated". This directs our attention back to verse 10 and 11, where we read, "Put on the whole armor of God that ye may be able to stand against the wiles of the devil." There is a distinct difference between how God presents this conflict to His children and how the devil does. God clearly spells out for us the power of our enemy, He points out the areas of concern and warns us to beware of his tactics. God exposes the devil in all his power and plans to the believer; the devil, on the other hand, does not dare to do the same for his followers. How could he? If he showed them the power and truth about God, there would be no one left to follow him! Rather, he lies and deceives, he blinds and denies concerning God. God has no need to do this because were there any weakness in God (which of course there is not), it would still be stronger than the power of the devil.

We see in verse 12 the "because clause", which gives us a clearer understanding about the nature of this issue. The first part of verse 12 presents the nature of this conflict that we are engaged in. It tells us here that we wrestle. Consider some principles that we can learn from this. First, there is this word "we", this includes all believers.

Paul, the great apostle, includes himself in this. No one is above the truth that each and every believer is bound to the conflict of the spiritual life. This includes the pastor and it includes the child on the church bus. There is no one who is exempt from this battle: we all wrestle. You do not get to choose if you will be in a spiritual fight. You do, however, get to choose at times if you are going to fight properly.

There are some who become too familiar with the enemy and play rather than engaging to destroy. They banter about, putting on the fashion of spiritual warfare, but they are not serious about winning the fight. Still others, rather than fighting the true enemy, seek to hinder others around them who are seeking to wage a good warfare, wrestling with their brethren rather than with the enemy, causing hindrances to the work of God from going forward and seeking to hold some others back from victories in their lives. There are again others who, rather than wrestling against the enemy, actually spend their time wrestling against the Lord. They won't submit to Him to be used by Him; they won't yield themselves as the Bible says that a believer should, and they don't present their bodies as living sacrifices unto God which is their reasonable service. Rather, they are always fighting against God transforming them into His image and wrestling against the Spirit. They are disobedient children who think that they know what is best for them, but all the while they are losing ground on where God has them going. Unfortunately, there are some who never seem to get out of these stages.

Everyone goes through some form of these stages in their young Christian life, but some refuse to mature and move forward; they are always acting immature. I remember when I was in the 7th grade, I tried out for the wrestling team. There was a boy around the corner from my house who was a bully. He would do things to hurt me and break my things whenever he had the chance. We were both in the same grade and we both 'went out for wrestling. I remember that as we practiced each day, learning about wrestling, I kept thinking, "I hope that they let me wrestle that guy! I am going to clean his clock." I want you to understand that I was not a great wrestler. As a matter of fact, I didn't really like wrestling. But the rule at home was once you start something, you have to finish it, so I was doing what I had to do to finish. I wrestled in a few matches but I hand't won any; I really was just going through the motions waiting for the end of the season. As we got to the end of the season, the time came for the last match. I finally had the opportunity to wrestle that guy. I was stoked up; I was going to whip him good! The match started and I took him down, twisted him up, and pinned him in the first round. I was so excited and yet my coach was not. As a matter of fact, he was rather disappointed in me. He said, "If you would have wrestled like that the rest of the year, you would have won all your matches." I was so intent on beating someone who was on my team that I neglected to beat anyone on any other team. There are so many Christians that are in that state, 'never realizing who the real opponent is. They are wrestling against themselves in reality and never maturing enough to get their eyes on the real enemy.

So we wrestle. Secondly, I want you to understand that this term "wrestle" is indicative of the fact that this is a single combat. Though we all are engaged in it, it is not a team sport. It is not me against a multitude; it is me against one enemy at a time. It isn't that Satan is just against all believers, as though we were all continually together. Brethren, I want you to know that he has specific designs on attacking you. Just like God longs to have a close intimate personal relationship with each one of His children, that is how the devil loves to attack, as well. Sometimes we can become so focused on the force of those standing around us that we forget that the enemy is intent on destroying us one by one.

Wrestling is a singular battle; it is one standing against another. When I was on that wrestling team, I had a whole team of guys sitting just feet was away from me. They were not, however, able to jump out there on the enemy and help me. No, I had to fight: just me and my opponent. Now, in truth, in this battle, the war is tilted in favor of the believer if he will exercise himself to it. For it is a battle between the devil and you, but there is someone who lives in you that is greater than your adversary and will by His power win the battle if you are yielded to Him.

I want you also to consider the intensity of this battle. In most sporting events, there is time between plays that gives you a chance to catch your breath. When you wrestle, you are stuck; there isn't a time out. It is you pushing with all your strength against another pushing with all their strength and it will wear you out quickly. There isn't a lot of running and jumping, but the nature of the exercise is such that it takes all your strength quickly. Spiritual wrestling is the same way; it doesn't take long to wear out your strength in such a match. There is a great amount of stamina that is required to prevail; you must not quit. You must push on regardless of how weary you are, because the moment that you let up you, will be pinned and lose the fight.

This is close intense combat. This is not like the army that sits at a safe distance and launches missiles at their enemy, never seeing first-hand until later the damage that they have caused. This is not like the sniper who sits aloft on his perch waiting for the singular moment that he might fire his weapon from afar. No, friend, this is personal; this is an intimate fight. You might likely get the other guys sweat in your eye. You are going to get your arms and legs locked together in combat so that others might not be able to readily discern where you end and they begin. You can run from someone that is shooting at you from a great distance, but you cannot run when they have you by the arm and leg.

I also want you to consider the continuation of this statement, "we wrestle." The tense of that phrase is never-ending. Meaning that the tense of it is not, "we will wrestle", or "we did wrestle", but, rather, that it is an active and ongoing process of conflict that we are engaged in. If you are saved, you have entered the match and you are engaged in it even today, whether you are persevering or not. I have been in the midst of a match that I thought would never end, and it seemed that the time keeper had forgotten to stop, so that it went on forever. I want you to know that as long as you are in this flesh, you are in the wrestling match with the enemy and it may seem that the clock will never stop. God is keeping time and score.

Before we move on, I want to consider two more thoughts on this. The statement does not end with the first three words: it says, "For we wrestle not against flesh and blood". In the next chapter, we are going to spend some time talking about who it is that we wrestle against, but first Paul gives us the negative to show us that it isn't a physical battle. It isn't a battle that can be won in the flesh. We wrestle not against flesh and blood. The weapons of our warfare are not carnal; this isn't a physical conflict at all. The problem is that we are so locked up in the thinking of the flesh. We are so consumed with the attributes of the flesh that we can hardly keep our attention on the true issues of the spirit. We are consumed with the physical and the problems are the spiritual.

Finally, let's consider that the statement "for we wrestle" is not a defensive statement, but rather an offensive one. In other words, if in wrestling you take only a defensive posture you will likely lose; it is not only about defending yourself, but rather attacking the opponent and seeking to pin them down. We were never intended by God to stand back and wait for the devil to attack us; rather, we are to be the ones on the attack. When you start to wrestle, they don't teach you how to be taken down; they teach you how to take down your opponent. They don't spend a lot of time teaching you on how to stay on your back, but rather, how to turn your opponent over and get on top. That is the battle strategy. When I wrestled, my best move was the neck bridge. I had that one down! I would get on my back and just keep my neck arched up so that they could not pin me, but brethren, that is not how you wrestle. That is the sign of an unskilled wrestler. The skillful wrestler is not just trying not to get pinned; the skillful wrestler is trying to win. We are not in this not to lose; we are in this to win! God has given us this battle to win! Whatever it is that you are engaged in fighting spiritually, God wants you to have victory! And that is what this passage is about: giving you the tools for victory. In order to do this, we must put on this armor that God is teaching us about. These are the tools of our craft, the weapons of our warfare. Let us determine not to sit back and be content to allow the devil to be the aggressor. Let us gird ourselves up and take the fight to him. We have been promised that the gates of hell would not prevail against us, meaning that if we are on the offensive, the devil has no defense against the weapons that God has outfitted us with.

# Nine

# *The Structure of the Enemy*

> Ephesians 6:12 For we wrestle not against flesh and blood, but against principalities, against powers, against the rulers of the darkness of this world, against spiritual wickedness in high *places*.

Over the last decade as a nation we have been involved in a war with an enemy unlike we have ever encountered before. The enemy is called radical Islam and it is constantly morphing and changing. It has a hierarchy but it is difficult to get a bead on. For a good deal of time, we thought that Osama Bin Laden was the head of it, but now as I read the news, it seems that there are many heads, or at least they cannot put a finger on one as the head. It is a network of shadows that slinks around in the darkness doing its destructive work. It would seem that it is able to even disguise itself enough to receive aid numerous times from the US, its sworn enemy. In many respects, though not all, this is like the nature of our spiritual enemy.

As we examine this verse, we will see some specific details about the enemy that God desires for us to take note of. First, we will consider the structure of our enemy, then in future chapters we will consider the strength of our enemy, the scope of our enemy, and then finally, the subtlety of our enemy.

As we consider the structure of our enemy, I want you to consider the opposition to the Lord as a vast army. The Bible says in

Revelation 12:3-4, "And there appeared another wonder in heaven; and behold a great red dragon, having seven heads and ten horns, and seven crowns upon his heads. And his tail drew the third part of the stars of heaven, and did cast them to the earth: and the dragon stood before the woman which was ready to be delivered, for to devour her child as soon as it was born."

The dragon here is a direct reference to Satan and the third of the stars is speaking of the angels that fell with him. So one third of the angels that were created are now fallen and demonic beings. These now make up the demonic opposition to God and His children. The head of this army is none other than the devil himself. As a matter of fact, the Bible calls him in John 14:30, "the prince of this world", and in Ephesians 2:2, "the prince of the power of the air, the spirit that now worketh in the children of disobedience:"

So Satan is the prince of this world; he is the ruler over those who are opposed to God, including the demonic angels that followed him and all men who reject God. Now he has an illegitimate kingdom that he stole from God, and God has a legitimate right to take it back. Though the devil is illegitimate in his reign, he maintains it by the willing subjection of those who refuse to receive Jesus Christ. Jesus said in John 8:44, "Ye are of *your* father the devil, and the lusts of your father ye will do. He was a murderer from the beginning, and abode not in the truth, because there is no truth in him. When he speaketh a lie, he speaketh of his own: for he is a liar, and the father of it."

Every prince has a throne, and so it is with the devil. It says in Revelation 2:12-13, "And to the angel of the church in Pergamos write; These things saith he which hath the sharp sword with two edges; I know thy works, and where thou dwellest, *even* where Satan's seat *is*: and thou holdest fast my name, and hast not denied my faith, even in those days wherein Antipas *was* my faithful martyr, who was slain among you, where Satan dwelleth." It is no small thing that the devil set up his throne in a church house. The devil loves to cloth himself in the robes of righteousness and imitate God.

It is the devil's ultimate goal to have men bow down and worship him, and during the tribulation that will happen. It says so in

Revelation 13:4: "And they worshipped the dragon which gave power unto the beast: and they worshipped the beast, saying, Who *is* like unto the beast? who is able to make war with him?" Until the devil gets men to bow down to him directly, he is quite content with them bowing down to anything that is not God. That is why he submits so many different religions and idolatries to men. That is why he entices men with all the lusts of the flesh: to keep their attention away from worshiping the one true God.

He rules in the hearts of men through his law which is opposed to the law of God. His is the law of sin. It says in Romans 7:18-25, "For I know that in me (that is, in my flesh,) dwelleth no good thing: for to will is present with me; but *how* to perform that which is good I find not. For the good that I would I do not: but the evil which I would not, that I do. Now if I do that I would not, it is no more I that do it, but sin that dwelleth in me. I find then a law, that, when I would do good, evil is present with me. For I delight in the law of God after the inward man: But I see another law in my members, warring against the law of my mind, and bringing me into captivity to the law of sin which is in my members. O wretched man that I am! who shall deliver me from the body of this death? I thank God through Jesus Christ our Lord. So then with the mind I myself serve the law of God; but with the flesh the law of sin." Paul goes on to say in Romans 8:2, "For the law of the Spirit of life in Christ Jesus hath made me free from the law of sin and death."

Now the Christian is free, then, from the law of sin through Jesus Christ, but the presence of that old law is still there. Imagine it like this: you grew up in a different culture with different laws and then you changed your citizenship to America. There is going to be some time of adjustment that takes place until your thinking is not affected by those old laws, but, likely some of them would remain with you forever. It will be a constant struggle to put away the old way of thinking from the old culture and adopt the new way of thinking from the new culture. The devil is always trying to exploit that old way of thinking and draw you back into the old nature, though you cannot be lost again. He would love for your walk with God to be hindered and for you to be a hindrance to others.

The devil even has substitute doctrines for you if you will accept them. It says in 1 Timothy 4:1-3, "Now the Spirit speaketh expressly, that in the latter times some shall depart from the faith, giving heed to seducing spirits, and doctrines of devils; Speaking lies in hypocrisy; having their conscience seared with a hot iron; Forbidding to marry, *and commanding* to abstain from meats, which God hath created to be received with thanksgiving of them which believe and know the truth."

The doctrines of the devil are intended to hinder, not help. They are intended to turn your heart away from truth, substituting a form of asceticism that denies the power of God and develops a self-righteous attitude.

We see that the forces of darkness have a prince who has a throne and is seeking worship. He has a law and he has his own doctrines. He also has an army, which is divided into a hierarchy. Just like any other army, there are generals and majors and captains and so on; there is an order to the demonic army, as well. The Bible speaks of regional princes in Daniel 10:20: "Then said he, Knowest thou wherefore I come unto thee? and now will I return to fight with the prince of Persia: and when I am gone forth, lo, the prince of Grecia shall come."

This was spoken by the angel Michael and if you notice he speaks of his conflict with the prince of Persia and then of the prince of Grecia. These were demonic forces that had been given designated authority over those regions. The Devil is over all the air and his generals, so to speak, are given authority over that region. Now remember the devil and his demons are not like God at all. God is omnipresent, there is not a single place that you can go that God is not already there. The devil and his angels are not that way; they are confined to a specific location just as you and I are and all the angels of God are. They can travel but they are restricted in that sense.

Likewise the devils differ from one another in strength. We will talk of that later; I am just saying that they are not all in a group running around the neighborhood beating people up and taking their lunch money. They are assigned to specific regions to accomplish their demonic purposes, working together as a vast networked army.

This being said, there are some good things to take note of from the scriptures that we have seen. Though a third of the angels fell and became followers of the devil, two thirds of the angels did not fall and are still the ministers of God. That means that on a numerical level, though we don't know the exact number of demonic forces there are, we know that they are already out numbered two to one. That is good to know! We also know that we have been given through Jesus Christ freedom from the law of the devil and his minions. Though they have rule over the sinful region around us, we are not bound by the law of sin, we are, as it says in Hebrews, strangers and pilgrims in this land. The law of sin does not apply to us; we are under a higher law. The throne of the devil has no ability to force the children of God to worship him who is illegitimate in his position, nor to hold to the doctrines that are opposed to the truth.

Child of God, knowing these things makes it all the more important that we submit ourselves to the rule of God in our lives. We are citizens of an opposing kingdom, and yet so often we are fraternizing with the enemy and flirting with the wickedness of this world. So let me ask you some specific and personal questions.

1. Who is on the throne of your heart? The natural man enthrones the works of the devil and gives allegiance to the old sin nature. However, when a person gets saved, they are to cast off the works of darkness and enthrone Jesus Christ in their life. That means that He is the King in your heart, that He is to be worshiped and adored. He is to be glorified and honored in all that you do. All too often, we spend our lives with our own desires and will on the throne, making our own decisions, and ruling our own lives. Then we blame God for the results. We do not humbly submit ourselves to the Word of God and His Spirit as the direct guide for all that we do; we do what we want and then ask God to bless it. If you have not dethroned self and sin in your life and give that place to God, then you are living a double life and giving aid and comfort to the enemy.

2. Whose law do you freely subject yourself to? We know that the law of sin is present in our members, but if you are saved, you also now have the law of holiness present in you. Do you find

yourself yielding more to the law of sin or the law of God? When there seems to be no pressure to do otherwise, are you more likely to subject yourself to spiritual endeavors or carnal?

3. Where do you run for protection? When the battle is hot, when you are pressed and feel the burden of life, do you run to the Lord and His Word? Do you resort to prayer or do you quickly give into the old lusts of the flesh? Is your sense of peace found in a close relationship to the Lord or in the comforts of the old actions? Who you resort to in times of distress will tell you who is really on the throne of your heart, revealing who is really getting victory in your life.

4. Who do you sympathize with? Your prince is the one whose victories and losses you take to heart. So when the Spirit of God speaks to you and asks you to give up some deed or even some relationship, do you mourn for the loss of that which you love or do you gladly cling to the Spirit of God in love? When the Word of God lays a commandment out before you, do you argue with God about the necessity of it or do you willingly grab hold of it and with joy practice it? Where do your sympathies lie, with the old flesh or with the new man?

The structure of the forces of darkness are laid out, their principalities and order are clear in the scriptures. Yet if you are a child of God, you are not bound by their structure, you are not under their authority, and their power is not confining for you.

Ten

# *The Strength of the Enemy*

We have established that the believer is in a conflict against three enemies of righteousness: the world, the flesh, and the devil. As we consider the strength of the enemy, we notice that the word used here to describe the enemy that we wrestle against is "powers". The word powers here means ability, force, or authority. There are some things that the devil has the ability, the strength, and the authority to do. These things, praise the Lord, are finite. He cannot do anything that he wants; he is still limited, though he is very powerful. Yet God has revealed the work of Satan and his power in the scriptures, so let's take a look at the strength and power that he does have.

There are three primary areas of influence that the devil has in this world. He can possess the lost, that is, he can indwell them and animate them to do works of darkness, as he did with many listed in the scripture that Jesus cast demons out of, such as the maniac of Gadera. He can oppress such as he did with Paul, as it says in 2 Corinthians 12:7. "And lest I should be exalted above measure through the abundance of the revelations, there was given to me a thorn in the flesh, the messenger of Satan to buffet me, lest I should be exalted above measure." The final level of working that he has is obsessing people, or in other words, getting them focused on him and his work rather than on God and His work. The devil tried to do this with Paul. In the book of Acts, it tells us that in a certain place a woman possessed with a devil followed Paul and cried out for days about him until he cast the devil out. The attempt was to get him focused on the devils rather than on the work of the gospel. Even as we study this passage and reveal the working of the devil, I want you to remember that our focus should never be on the devil, but rather on the work of God. We are studying this to help us to better fight the spiritual battle, not just for the information of it.

So I want to take a study for a few minutes to reveal areas the Bible says that the devil has strength or power. The Bible says in Ephesians 2:2, "Wherein in time past ye walked according to the course of this world, according to the prince of the power of the air, the spirit that now worketh in the children of disobedience:" Take note of these and the verses that reveal some of the powers of the devil.

The devil has the power to deceive. It says in Revelation 12:9, "And the great dragon was cast out, that old serpent, called the Devil, and Satan, which deceiveth the whole world: he was cast out into the earth, and his angels were cast out with him." We have already examined how the devil deceived Eve, but this verse tells us that one day he will deceive the whole world, meaning all that are not God's. That day has not yet come; there is still hope for those who are not yet saved, but there will come a time that multitudes will, under the deception of Satan, stand to fight against God and will, because of their sin, be destroyed with him.

The devil has the power to physically afflict. It says in Revelation 2:10, "Fear none of those things which thou shalt suffer: behold, the devil shall cast *some* of you into prison, that ye may be tried; and ye shall have tribulation ten days: be thou faithful unto death, and I will give thee a crown of life." We see this physical affliction demonstrated in both those who believed in and trusted God as well as in those who were lost. Job was physically afflicted, though he believed in God. The devil was able to inflict him with boils from the top of his head to the bottom of his feet. We also read already that Paul had a messenger of Satan in his flesh. While the devil cannot afflict a believer without consent from God, we see that God will allow this to test us, as in the case of Job, or to keep us humble as in the case of Paul. The Gospels are filled with illustrations of lost men who were physically affected by the devil. One of the most memorable accounts is that of the maniac of Gadera. The devils that afflicted him caused him to cut himself and repeatedly inflict physical harm to himself. Another illustration of this is the boy whose father came to the disciples because he was possessed; the Bible says that the devils would cast him into the flames. Remember, however, in all these cases of lost men, Christ cast the demonic influence out of the individuals. The Devil is stronger than a man, but it is not stronger than Jesus Christ.

The Devil has power to persecute, as we see in Psalm 7:5. "Let the enemy persecute my soul, and take *it*; yea, let him tread down my life upon the earth, and lay mine honour in the dust. Selah." And in Psalm 143:3, "For the enemy hath persecuted my soul; he hath smitten my life down to the ground; he hath made me to dwell in darkness, as those that have been long dead." The scriptures here do not say an enemy, but "the enemy". The enemy of the believer is the devil who loves to persecute the people of God.

The Devil has power to oppress, as we notice in Psalm 42:9, "I will say unto God my rock, Why hast thou forgotten me? why go I mourning because of the oppression of the enemy?" David was greatly oppressed by the devil, causing him to be depressed and even question if God had forgotten him. God had not forgotten David and neither does God forget you when you are under a time of oppression. Rather, these are times that prove us and cause us to purify our hearts and minds so that we might have a better relationship with God than we have had before.

The devil has the power to bring reproach on us according to Psalm 74:10, "O God, how long shall the adversary reproach? shall the enemy blaspheme thy name for ever?" The devil loves to try and cause God and His people to be reproached in this world and the world is ever eager to believe a bad report about the Christian. God, however, has promised us that the truth will prevail. The lies of the devil will lose in the end and God will expose him for what he is, a liar and deceiver.

The devil has the power to tempt. He did this very thing to Jesus in Matthew 4:1, "Then was Jesus led up of the Spirit into the wilderness to be tempted of the devil." Jesus willingly submitted Himself to the temptation of the devil so that He might be able, as our high priest, to make intercession for us, having experienced all the temptations of this weak and feeble flesh, yet without having succumbed to the temptation. Unfortunately we have all fallen to the power of the tempter more often than we can count.

The devil has the power to steal the word from the heart of men. It says in Luke 8:12, "Those by the way side are they that hear; then cometh the devil, and taketh away the word out of their hearts, lest they should believe and be saved." The lost are often very willing to have the Word of God stolen from their heart, but let's not neglect the fact that the devil is active in trying to keep people from trusting Christ as their Savior. He loves to divert the attention of men who are hearing the gospel so that they will not respond in obedience to Christ. Often in witnessing to someone, I have been amazed at the strange things that will occur just at the moment of them making a decision. That is not a coincidence; it is the thief coming to steal the Word from them.

The devil has power to suggest evil deeds to men. He did just that in John 13:2, "And supper being ended, the devil having now put into the heart of Judas Iscariot, Simon's *son*, to betray him;" Judas was a willing accomplice, but the idea to betray Jesus to His death was the suggestion of Satan. Judas 'isn't the only one who has ever been influenced by the demonic suggestion to do evil. Satan uses his power as often as he can to hinder men and hurt the work of God from going forward.

The devil has power to condemn in this world. Praise God he has no power beyond this world, but in this world, he loves to draw the man of God into temptation and then expose the sin to bring condemnation and disgrace to the people of God. It says in 1 Timothy 3:6, speaking of the qualification of a pastor that he should be an experienced man at walking with God, "Not a novice, lest being lifted up with pride he fall into the condemnation of the devil."

The devil has power to devour those who fall away in their walk with God. It says in 1 Peter 5:8, "Be sober, be vigilant; because your adversary the devil, as a roaring lion, walketh about, seeking whom he may devour:". The word devour here has nothing to do with loosing salvation, but rather with being overcome and becoming useless in this life to serve God as we should have. Many have been devoured and have been unable to do what they could have done for God because they were not watching against the attack of Satan in their life.

The devil has the power to infiltrate God's house. There is a host of scripture to back up this claim. Consider the following verses.

> Psalm 74:3 "Lift up thy feet unto the perpetual desolations; *even* all *that* the enemy hath done wickedly in the sanctuary."
>
> Matthew 13:25 "But while men slept, his enemy came and sowed tares among the wheat, and went his way."
>
> Matthew 13:28 "He said unto them, An enemy hath done this. The servants said unto him, Wilt thou then that we go and gather them up?"
>
> Matthew 13:39 "The enemy that sowed them is the devil; the harvest is the end of the world; and the reapers are the angels."
>
> John 6:70 "Jesus answered them, Have not I chosen you twelve, and one of you is a devil?"
>
> Acts 13:10 "And said, O full of all subtilty and all mischief, *thou* child of the devil, *thou* enemy of all righteousness, wilt thou not cease to pervert the right ways of the Lord?"

We have noted before that revelation tells us that Satan has a seat in one of the seven churches listed there. I would submit that he does his best work from inside the church house. We are to be always watching and vigilant. The moment that we think that we cannot be infiltrated by the devil's sly ways we are prone to just that. He doesn't come in as an attacker; he comes in as an angel of light. He comes in and seems so spiritual that he could not be picked out by most. He comes in and begins to sow his seeds of destruction ever so lightly and is so deceptive that he gets people on his side time and time again so that when he is revealed many are drawn away in shame.

The devil has the power over death. It says in Hebrews 2:14-15, "Forasmuch then as the children are partakers of flesh and blood, he also himself likewise took part of the same; that through death he might destroy him that had the power of death, that is, the devil; And deliver them who through fear of death were all their lifetime subject to bondage." E. Schuyler English (Studies in the Epistle to the Hebrews, p. 82) says of this verse, "The Law of God demanded and does demand death for sin. 'The soul that sinneth, it shall die.' 'The wages of sin is death.' Satan was the cause of man's sin in the first place and, even though he is a usurper, he can claim, justly so in a sense, that the sinner must die. He had the power, the authority to demand that every sinner should pay sin's penalty. And on account of this all men, because all are sinners, were fearful of death and subject to bondage, because of sin, to serve it and thus serve Satan."

During the tribulation, the power that the devil has will be greatly increased so that he will be able to do significantly more than he is able to do now, being restrained by the presence of the Holy Spirit on this earth through the children of God. However, I also want you to remember that the power of the devil is, without doubt, illegitimate, as we have said, and thus, God has the right to override the plans and will of the devil. Jesus said in Matthew 28:18-20, "And Jesus came and spake unto them, saying, All power is given unto me in heaven and in earth. Go ye therefore, and teach all nations, baptizing them in the name of the Father, and of the Son, and of the Holy Ghost: Teaching them to observe all things whatsoever I have commanded you: and, lo, I am with you alway, *even* unto the end of the world. Amen."

One passage that gives me great hope is found in Luke 10:17-19, "And the seventy returned again with joy, saying, Lord, even the devils are subject unto us through thy name. And he said unto them, I beheld Satan as lightning fall from heaven. Behold, I give unto you power to tread on serpents and scorpions, and over all the power of the enemy: and nothing shall by any means hurt you." God has given His children the ability to use His power. The problem is that we often neglect to do so. At one point, God allowed the devil to oppress me in a severe way. I was under a heavy load of guilt and physically was affected by the weight that the accuser was piling on me. I found it hard to get up and go; I even felt as though I had a weight sitting on my chest so that it was hard to breath. It seemed that every day I was praying, "Lord, please help me", but every day it was getting worse. One morning I got up early and was sitting in my living room, I told the Lord that if He didn't give me something to help me I didn't think that I was going to make it. I opened my Bible up and read this passage in Luke 10. It was as though God said, "All you have to do is command them to depart. I have given you the access to my authority." Now I couldn't believe what I was reading, was this the answer? So I prayed, "Lord, please tell the demonic oppression to depart", but God said no to my spirit. I didn't understand and as I kept reading I realized what God was trying to get me to see. He had given me the authority through His name to command the demonic presence to depart but I was responsible to do it.

Consider it like this. I was asking Him to do what He had given me authority to do already. He wanted me to act by faith to exercise the authority that He had given. I considered that for a time. I am not saying that we have the authority of God to go and command all demons to do whatever we want, please understand. But if God speaking to us through His Word impresses on us to command an oppressive demonic force to depart, we have the authority to do that. The power is not in us, it is in God's name and in His Word. I called out in this way and immediately the heavy oppressive spirit lifted from off me as if it were a curtain being drawn up. Can you understand that the devils are far more powerful that you, but they are not more powerful that God! If you exercise the command of the Word of God they must obey God.

So the power of Jesus Christ is far greater than that of the devil. Consider it to be like comparing the strength of a child to that of a strong man. The child has some strength and can accomplish some things, but he is no match against the strength of a man. So the Bible declares in Colossians 1:13, "Who hath delivered us from the power of darkness, and hath translated *us* into the kingdom of his dear Son:". The power of God supersedes and overrides the power of the devil, and the dominion of Satan cannot withstand against the power of God.

That power was given also to the Children of God to exercise in doing the work of God. It says in Matthew 10:1, "And when he had called unto *him* his twelve disciples, he gave them power *against* unclean spirits, to cast them out, and to heal all manner of sickness and all manner of disease." Mark 3:15 tells us, "And to have power to heal sicknesses, and to cast out devils: in Mark 6:7, "And he called *unto him* the twelve, and began to send them forth by two and two; and gave them power over unclean spirits;"

When Jesus was being crucified He said to Pilate in John 19:11, "Jesus answered, Thou couldest have no power *at all* against me, except it were given thee from above: therefore he that delivered me unto thee hath the greater sin." It tells us in Romans 13:1, "Let every soul be subject unto the higher powers. For there is no power but of God: the powers that be are ordained of God."

Someday, the Lord is going to nullify all the power that was allowed to the workers of darkness and destroy them, as it says in 1 Corinthians 15:24, "Then *cometh* the end, when he shall have delivered up the kingdom to God, even the Father; when he shall have put down all rule and all authority and power." It tells us in Ephesians 1:20-23, "Which he wrought in Christ, when he raised him from the dead, and set *him* at his own right hand in the heavenly *places*, Far above all principality, and power, and might, and dominion, and every name that is named, not only in this world, but also in that which is to come: And hath put all *things* under his feet, and gave him *to be* the head over all *things* to the church, Which is his body, the fulness of him that filleth all in all."

Jesus Christ is far above the principality of the devil and the power of the devil, and God supersedes the structure and the strength of the darkness of the devil, and thus, we have no need to fear the devil. We do have need to be watchful, and we do have need to be diligent in our walk and our warfare. There is a great danger for the individual that is not walking with God. The devil is mightier than your flesh and will destroy you and it, if possible, but He cannot do anything against the Spirit of God.

# Eleven

# *The Scope of the Enemy*

> Ephesians 6:12 "For we wrestle not against flesh and blood, but against principalities, against powers, against the rulers of the darkness of this world, against spiritual wickedness in high *places*."

As we move on to the third portion of this verse considering the nature of the enemy, we will notice the phrase, "against the rulers of the darkness of this world". In this phrase, we find the scope of the enemies' rule, meaning the amount that it covers. Here we find three primary things that are wonderful to note as a believer about the scope of the devil's authority and rule.

Notice that the scope of the devils rule is limited in time. The scripture here says that it is limited to this world. The devil does not have an eternity to ply his trade; no, he is limited in his time. The Bible says in 1 Corinthians 15:24-25, "Then *cometh* the end, when he shall have delivered up the kingdom to God, even the Father; when he shall have put down all rule and all authority and power. For he must reign, till he hath put all enemies under his feet." The end of the rule of darkness will come and suddenly as a thief in the night, the devil does not know the time of his end, but he knows that the time is coming when God intends on putting all things back under His rule as they were in the beginning and as they were intended to be. There are two things to consider as you think about the time limit of the devil's rule.

First, the rulers of darkness know that they have but a short time, as it says in Revelation 12:12, "Therefore rejoice, *ye* heavens, and ye that dwell in them. Woe to the inhabiters of the earth and of the sea! for the devil is come down unto you, having great wrath, because he knoweth that he hath but a short time." Thus, as they know this to be the case, they are fevered to accomplish their vile tasks. They have nothing to lose; in essence, there is no place of repentance for them. There is no hope of redemption, thus they are content only in indulging themselves in as much wickedness and ungodliness as they possibly can before their ultimate torment begins. Remember the devil will not rule over hell. The Bible declares in Matthew 25:41, "Then shall he say also unto them on the left hand, Depart from me, ye cursed, into everlasting fire, prepared for the devil and his angels:"

The lake of fire was prepared for the torment and judgment of the devil and his angels. He will not rule there; he will suffer there and so will all the demons that follow him. Men and women who likewise reject God have no better thing to look forward to than to fill their hearts and minds with the lusts of the flesh, for this is as good as it will get for them. There is a certain fiery judgment that awaits all the forces of darkness and their time is limited. Is it any wonder that the world spins further and further into debauchery, seemingly at a faster rate every day? The law of sin, which they serve, cannot be satisfied or quenched by the indulgence of it. They are spiraling out of control on their way to their ultimate doom.

However, for the Believer, there is also a thought here. As a matter of fact, I tell you, friend, this is a great blessing to know! No matter how hard the battle is today, no matter how weary we get, we know that the devil's time is limited. We are told in Titus 2:12-13, "Teaching us that, denying ungodliness and worldly lusts, we should live soberly, righteously, and godly, in this present world; Looking for that blessed hope, and the glorious appearing of the great God and our Saviour Jesus Christ;"

As we have studied this passage about the nature of the enemy, I find this to be one of the most encouraging thoughts that I have encountered. The devil is finite in his time. His time is coming, his hour is almost over, and the reward of his wickedness is about due. Someone once rightly said, "When Satan reminds you of your past, remind him of his future." He may rule the darkness of this world, but it will only be in this world, and this world is quickly coming to an end.

The second aspect of the scope of the enemy that we see is the place of his rule, which is also this world. That is this world here below. He has no rule in heaven, the highest the devil can go is the air, and he is called the prince of the power of the air. He was expelled from the Holy abode of God; he has no place there now at all. There is no room reserved for him; there is no expectation or reservation that is left for him in Heaven. However, we who are saved have such reservations. Our Jesus said that He went to prepare us a place. The place for the devil has already been prepared; the place that he has gone to prepare for us has been 2000 years in the making. The best that the rule of the devil will ever do is to rule down here. He is a prince of this world only, however, in Christ Jesus, we are made kings in the next world.

Were we as afflicted in this life by the attack of the devil as Job, we would still have such a great promise that we could not fail, and, as Job could still declare, Job 19:25-27, "For I know *that* my redeemer liveth, and *that* he shall stand at the latter *day* upon the earth: And *though* after my skin *worms* destroy this *body*, yet in my flesh shall I see God: Whom I shall see for myself, and mine eyes shall behold, and not another; *though* my reins be consumed within me."

Here, we are strangers and pilgrims. The more that I study this passage, the more real that thought has become to me. The problem that we have is that we have attached ourselves to this present world, it is as though this was our kingdom, as well. What is here to hold us? What is here for us to long for? Do we not have a better city promised? Is there not a better King for us to follow? The rulers of this world have done a woeful job and have brought destruction, misery, and death as the reward of their reign, but our King gives peace and joy and life! This world then is not our home; we are just passing through. The reason that Satan fights so hard to retain his place here on this earth is that this is all he has. The believer has much more if they will lay claim to it. We should not have our eyes set upon things below. Paul said it, as well, in Colossians 3:1-2, "If ye then be risen with Christ, seek those things which are above, where Christ sitteth on the right hand of God. Set your affection on things above, not on things on the earth."

The third aspect that we see in this passage in regard to the scope of the enemy is the subjects that follow him. It says here that he rules over the darkness of this world, meaning that he rules over all those who are in darkness in this world. The Bible speaks of these in many places, as in Isaiah 50:10, "Who *is* among you that feareth the LORD, that obeyeth the voice of his servant, that walketh *in* darkness, and hath no light? let him trust in the name of the LORD, and stay upon his God." In Ephesians 5:11, we are commanded, "And have no fellowship with the unfruitful works of darkness, but rather reprove *them*." Before we were saved, we were categorized by God as in darkness, as it says in Ephesians 5:8, "For ye were sometimes darkness, but now *are ye* light in the Lord: walk as children of light:"

There are two aspects to consider in regard to this darkness. First, the works of darkness, and secondly, the state of darkness. As we consider the works of darkness, we understand that all sin is a product of the darkness. There is no such thing as righteous sin, when we sin, we are, in fact, engaging in the works of darkness: the lusts of the flesh and the deeds of Satan. That is why God warns us so vehemently in the Bible to abstain from all the works of the flesh, and to mortify our members which are in Christ. We are told by Paul in Romans 6:12, "Let not sin therefore reign in your mortal body, that ye should obey it in the lusts thereof." Christian, when you allow sin to reign in your body, you are making yourself a willing servant in the flesh to the devil. You are saying that you, indeed, will serve the father of sin. How can a child of God make such a willful decision? We should understand that as a child of God, we cannot live in the lust of the flesh. To do so is to betray our King and give allegiance to the ruler of the darkness.

As a matter of fact, I believe that we should examine ourselves whether we are too in love with the works of darkness and then claim that we are in the light. Jesus said in John 3:19, "And this is the condemnation, that light is come into the world, and men loved darkness rather than light, because their deeds were evil." Paul told us in Romans 13:12, "The night is far spent, the day is at hand: let us therefore cast off the works of darkness, and let us put on the armour of light." John three times warned about the deceitfulness of the works of darkness when He said in 1 John 1:6, "If we say that we have fellowship with him, and walk in darkness, we lie, and do not the truth:" And in 1 John 2:9, "He that saith he is in the light, and hateth his brother, is in darkness even until now." And then again in 1 John 2:11, "But he that hateth his brother is in darkness, and walketh in darkness, and knoweth not whither he goeth, because that darkness hath blinded his eyes."

Jesus warned us Luke 11:35, too, "Take heed therefore that the light which is in thee be not darkness." And then said in, Matthew 6:23, "But if thine eye be evil, thy whole body shall be full of darkness. If therefore the light that is in thee be darkness, how great *is* that darkness!" He said, as well, in John 8:12, "Then spake Jesus again unto them, saying, I am the light of the world: he that followeth me shall not walk in darkness, but shall have the light of life."

You see when a person gets saved, the Bible says in 1 Peter 2:9, "But ye *are* a chosen generation, a royal priesthood, an holy nation, a peculiar people; that ye should shew forth the praises of him who hath called you out of darkness into his marvellous light:" Then things change; 1 Thessalonians 5:5 shows us, "Ye are all the children of light, and the children of the day: we are not of the night, nor of darkness." Instead, the Bible says that God has, according to Colossians 1:13, "Who hath delivered us from the power of darkness, and hath translated *us* into the kingdom of his dear Son:"

So we are free from the works of darkness if we are in Christ Jesus. We should not be satisfied to dwell in them; the Holy Ghost, rather, in our hearts, should be moving us to flee from them and escape their devastating grasp.

The second aspect to consider in regard to the darkness is the state of darkness, that place in which Jesus finds the lost man. Remember that Jesus is the Light, declaring in Matthew 4:16, "The people which sat in darkness saw great light; and to them which sat in the region and shadow of death light is sprung up." He said also in John 12:46, "I am come a light into the world, that whosoever believeth on me should not abide in darkness." The reason that He came was clearly shown in Acts 26:18, "To open their eyes, *and* to turn *them* from darkness to light, and *from* the power of Satan unto God, that they may receive forgiveness of sins, and inheritance among them which are sanctified by faith that is in me."

Every one that believes upon Him is given the light of the Lord Jesus Christ within their hearts, as it says in 2 Corinthians 4:6 ,"For God, who commanded the light to shine out of darkness, hath shined in our hearts, to *give* the light of the knowledge of the glory of God in the face of Jesus Christ."

The darkness must flee before the light, though it may feel as though it encroaches upon us. The more that we shine the light of the Word of God abroad in our hearts, the less darkness the ruler of the darkness has to work with. It should be the earnest desire of each and every believer to cast off the darkness in their hearts, as well as to shine the light of the glory of God to every subject of the devil's rule to diminish the scope of his rule and expand the kingdom of our God.

Twelve

# *The Subtlety of the Enemy*

> Ephesians 6:12 For we wrestle not against flesh and blood, but against principalities, against powers, against the rulers of the darkness of this world, against spiritual wickedness in high *places*.

As we have looked at Ephesians 6:12, we've noticed two major divisions. First, we saw the nature of the conflict that we face as believers. Then we have spent the last several chapters taking a look at the nature of the enemy. We learned about the structure of the enemy that is seen in the description of "principalities". We learned about the strength of the enemy, as seen in the term "powers". We then looked at the scope of the enemy, as it tells us about "the rulers of the darkness of this world", Now, we are going to look at the subtlety of the enemy we find in the last phrase, "spiritual wickedness in high places".

Let's consider some aspects of the nature of our enemy that we have not yet explored by first considering the word "spiritual" in this phrase. There are two levels of existence that were created by God, the physical and the spiritual. The Bible tells us that God through Jesus Christ transcended these, existing in both completely at the same time. The scriptures clearly teach us in John 4:24, "God *is* a Spirit: and they that worship him must worship *him* in spirit and in truth." Yet God also came in the flesh and dwelt among men as Jesus Christ. Jesus was not half man half God; He was 100% God and 100% man at the same time. The very price of our salvation demanded this to be so, as it says in 1 Peter 3:18, "For Christ also hath once suffered for sins, the just for the unjust, that he might bring us to God, being put to death in the flesh, but quickened by the Spirit:"

God created man to dwell in both of these planes, as He created us in His image with a body, soul and spirit. The body anchors us to this physical world. The spirit, when it is alive through the regenerating power of the Holy Ghost, anchors us to the spiritual world, and the soul is the tether between the two. The soul of man makes the determination and decision of whether we will obey the physical or the spiritual man. The lost man does not have that option because as it says in Ephesians 2:1, "And you *hath he quickened*, who were dead in trespasses and sins;" The spiritual option of the lost man is void, being available for use by any spirit since it is not submitted to the Spirit of God.

The devil and demons are spirit beings and not physical. The Bible says so in Ephesians 2:2, "Wherein in time past ye walked according to the course of this world, according to the prince of the power of the air, the spirit that now worketh in the children of disobedience:" While they exist only on the spiritual plane, they work in the physical plane, as well. The difference between these two planes is that the spiritual can see the physical, but the physical is blind to the spiritual. This is illustrated for us in several passages of the scriptures, first in Numbers 22:31, "Then the LORD opened the eyes of Balaam, and he saw the angel of the LORD standing in the way, and his sword drawn in his hand: and he bowed down his head, and fell flat on his face."

As well in 2 Kings 6:17, "And Elisha prayed, and said, LORD, I pray thee, open his eyes, that he may see. And the LORD opened the eyes of the young man; and he saw: and, behold, the mountain *was* full of horses and chariots of fire round about Elisha." Now, the spiritual plane is greater than the physical, but the physical is often oblivious to the spiritual. Even as believers, we most often live as though the physical was all there was and ignore the necessity of our spiritual life.

Because the spiritual plane is invisible to the physical eye, there is a great subtlety to it. The devil and/or devils work with great impunity, for the most part, in the physical realm, able to speak to and through men unseen. As it was with Peter in Mark 8:31-33, "And he began to teach them, that the Son of man must suffer many things, and be rejected of the elders, and *of* the chief priests, and scribes, and be killed, and after three days rise again. And he spake that saying openly. And Peter took him, and began to rebuke him. But when he had turned about and looked on his disciples, he rebuked Peter, saying, Get thee behind me, Satan: for thou savourest not the things that be of God, but the things that be of men." Even though Peter walked with Jesus and loved Jesus, the devil was able to speak to him to the point that he reiterated the very words of the devil to Jesus as if they were his own. Another good example of this is Job's wife, when she said in Job 2:9, "Then said his wife unto him, Dost thou still retain thine integrity? curse God, and die."

Do you think that every thought you think is your own? Do you not see that devils can speak, though not on this physical plane? They can, and do, speak to the soul of men to affect and influence the thinking and decisions of men, just as the Spirit of God speaks to the heart of men to call and direct us. So, too, do devils speak to pervert and discourage. Consider again that Paul warned us in 2 Corinthians 10:3-6, "For though we walk in the flesh, we do not war after the flesh: (For the weapons of our warfare *are* not carnal, but mighty through God to the pulling down of strong holds;) Casting down imaginations, and every high thing that exalteth itself against the knowledge of God, and bringing into captivity every thought to the obedience of Christ; And having in a readiness to revenge all disobedience, when your obedience is fulfilled."

The devil tempts toward the indulgence of the flesh and the lusts of it so that he might keep our attention on this earthly physical plane so we might be willingly ignorant of the power of the spiritual plane. God explains the levels in Hebrews 2:6-9, "But one in a certain place testified, saying, What is man, that thou art mindful of him? or the son of man, that thou visitest him? Thou madest him a little lower than the angels; thou crownedst him with glory and honour, and didst set him over the works of thy hands: Thou hast put all things in subjection under his feet. For in that he put all in subjection under him, he left nothing *that is* not put under him. But now we see not yet all things put under him. But we see Jesus, who was made a little lower than the angels for the suffering of death, crowned with glory and honour; that he by the grace of God should taste death for every man."

So the physical is lower than the spiritual plane in power and ability. This is how the devil is able to influence the physical so easily; he is unseen to it and the natural man, though he knows within his heart that there is a spiritual plane, is fearful of it and seeks primarily to ignore it. The devil takes full advantage of this by seeking to make the spiritual plane mystical and scary to bring confusion and disillusion to the mind of men, keeping them from a true and full understanding. This allows him to work in the shadows of the unknown to men and influence the affairs of men with impunity and subtlety.

The devil seeks to fill the lost and saved with the indulgence of the flesh and obstruction of the view of the spiritual. His subtle attack doesn't care, however, if you are filled up with the indulgence of the sin of commission or the sin of spiritual pride over your omission of certain sins. There are many, both lost and saved, who have fallen prey to the subtle diversion of spiritual pride, which is no less spiritually wicked than the grossest commission of sin. How dare we live in such a state filled with the same sin that caused the devil to be cast out of heaven? It was pride that was his downfall, he sought to set up his own throne to be worshiped, and thus, he seeks men to do as well. He desires for all men to be filled up with their own goodness, whether it is because they believe that they are just good people and don't need Jesus Christ, or that they believe that because of their religious piety that they are better than everyone else, sitting in judgment against others, comparing others not to the grace of our Lord Jesus Christ, but to their own established standard of goodness that they have made. "I abstain from alcohol and therefore anyone who doesn't is beneath me," they express by the prideful air of their countenance. Truly, God would have all to do so, but to be prideful over such a thing is just as much sin as to indulge in it. Substitute anything that you like. Whatever is it that you abstain from that if someone would come and say, "show me a proof that you are a Christian," you would point to. "I do this" or

"I don't do that" means nothing but spiritual pride. The only evidence that is found before God that is acceptable is that the blood of Jesus Christ has been applied to the vast account of my sin. There is nothing good that I have done to deserve God's only Son I point to, neither before nor after my conversion.

How is it that you are so lifted up with pride in your spiritual superiority thou wicked man? Have you forgotten that it is not by works of righteousness but by His mercy that you are saved? Are you so bewitched like the Galatians that having begun in faith you are now pointing to your own goodness as the standard of your evidence in Christ? Are you now justified more than others because you are so righteous by your abstinence from the very things that others who are not even saved abstain from every day, as well? There are many lost men who do not commit such sins as you abstain from each day. How does your abstinence from them make you any better than they are? Truly, we are to withdraw ourselves from every work of darkness, but not to add righteousness, rather because the Spirit of God living in us teaches us to deny ungodliness. If it is, then, His teaching in us, how do we claim any credit for it at all? Should we not, rather, be even more humbled by the extent of His grace to bring us daily into the Light of His countenance instead of being lifted up in spiritual pride? But this is nothing other than the subtle work of the devil to beguile us into spiritual wickedness.

Further, as we consider the subtle nature of the enemy, I want you to consider also, regarding this phrase, "spiritual wickedness in high places", that the primary goal of the devil is to pervert that which is God's, seeking to counterfeit all truly spiritual things. One such glaring example was given recently in an article published by the Independent on September 11, 2013, when they reported the following, "Responding to a list of questions published in the paper by Mr Scalfari, who is not a Roman Catholic, Francis wrote: "'You ask me if the God of the Christians forgives those who don't believe and who don't seek the faith. I start by saying – and this is the fundamental thing – that God's mercy has no limits if you go to him with a sincere and contrite heart. The issue for those who do not believe in God is to obey their conscience. Sin, even for those who have no faith, exists when people disobey their conscience."

Now the Pope, whoever he was, has always stood for and promoted an unbiblical view of salvation. However, here we have another example of spiritual wickedness in high places subtly destroying the truth of the Word of God. Nowhere in the Bible would you find such drivel. The Bible clearly says in 1 John 3:4, "Whosoever committeth sin transgresseth also the law: for sin is the transgression of the law." The idea that sin is simply violating your own conscience is setting every man up as his own law and nullifying the law of God. It is interesting how in tune the Pope is with another so-called spiritual leader, Joel Olsteen, who had this interaction in an interview with Larry King on June 20, 2005.

> "KING: What if you're Jewish or Muslim, you don't accept Christ at all?
>
> OSTEEN: You know, I'm very careful about saying who would and wouldn't go to heaven. I don't know ...
> KING: If you believe you have to believe in Christ? They're wrong, aren't they?
>
> OSTEEN: Well, I don't know if I believe they're wrong. I believe here's what the Bible teaches and from the Christian faith this is what I believe. But I just think that only God with judge a person's heart. I spent a lot of time in India with my father. I don't know all about their religion. But I know they love God. And I don't know. I've seen their sincerity. So I don't know. I know for me, and what the Bible teaches, I want to have a relationship with Jesus."

So the Pope says just follow your conscience and you will go to heaven, and Joel Olsteen says as long as you're sincere, it doesn't matter if you are a Christian, Hindu, Jew or Muslim, it will all be okay. What you see in these examples is spiritual wickedness in high places. These men are not just misguided; they have been fed a line by devils that they are repeating and, in fact, deceiving multitudes into believing that they actually speak for God.

The same spiritual wickedness in high places occurs in every false religion on the face of this world, be it Muslim, Hindu, Buddhist, Bahia, Scientology, Mormon, Jehovah's Witness, or any other that you might name, including the social gospel of the modern Protestant and Non-Denominational movements. There are lies upon lies that are told in the name of gods to deceive men and satisfy their soul's natural desire to reach out to God by handing them substitute gods and elevating men who will speak lies to deceive them. The average person is greatly confused by the whole thing. Knocking doors recently, I spoke to a man who said that he was interested in all spiritual things including the Bible and the Koran. These are opposed to one another, but the modern spiritual wickedness in our world has placed them on the same level. Yet Jesus Christ still says in, John 14:6, "Jesus saith unto him, I am the way, the truth, and the life: no man cometh unto the Father, but by me."

Listen to me today. There is no other way to have a relationship with God than through Jesus Christ. There is no other plan; there is no other method. You can be sincere about what you believe all the way to Hell, you can obey your conscience all the way to Hell, you can exercise yourself into false religious spirituality all the way to Hell, but you cannot get to Heaven any other way except through Jesus Christ, by faith in His shed blood on Calvary, His death, burial and resurrection. This is the only way of salvation.

DO THYSELF NO HARM

Thirteen

# *Developing Tactical Awareness: Identifying the Access Points*

One of the greatest threats to a soldier is not being aware of his own weaknesses. We are told repeatedly in the Bible to be watchful. The Webster's 1828 dictionary defines watchful as: "To be attentive; to be vigilant in preparation for an event or trial, the time of whose arrival is uncertain; to tend; to guard." In the military, this is known as tactical awareness. A soldier who is not watchful is more likely to fall victim to the enemy. Likewise, we as believers are to be watchful against our enemy. To do this, we must identify the areas of weakness that we have and remove them. What I mean is that we must evaluate ourselves to see where the access points are that the Devil could use to infiltrate our thinking and influence us.

This idea of access points is what Ephesians 4:1-6:9 deals with. Here is another way to think of it, imagine a house, each door and window are potential points of entry. If you leave the front door or garage door open, it is much easier for an intruder to come in. In each room there are windows that may be left open or unlocked which would give access to a thief. Your life is quite like this; you have many access points that you can open or close based on your involvement in them. If you close them, the Devil does not have access there. But if you open them, you give the Devil an opportunity or a place to cause you problems.

> Ephesians 4:27 "Neither give place to the devil."

Your next assignment is to read through Ephesians 4:1-6:9 and identify the access points that they warn about. These access points can be seen in two different ways.

1. Things we don't do that we should.
2. Things we do that we shouldn't.

Let me give you a few illustrations so you have a good idea of what you're looking for.

> Ephesians 4:1-3 "I therefore, the prisoner of the Lord, beseech you that ye walk worthy of the vocation wherewith ye are called, With all lowliness and meekness, with longsuffering, forbearing one another in love; Endeavouring to keep the unity of the Spirit in the bond of peace."

These verses are talking about things that we are supposed to do as believers. Not doing these things would potentially provide an access point to the Devil. Based upon this, I will list a few access points that we see here.

1. Not walking worthy of my calling as a believer. – vs. 1
2. Having pride – the opposite of lowliness and meekness – vs. 2
3. Being impatient – the opposite of longsuffering and forbearing – vs. 2
4. Not loving one another – vs. 2
5. Being contentious or causing strife – the opposite of unity and peace – vs. 3

Do you see how not doing these things that we have been called to do as believers would give access to the Devil to influence us? Now let me give you a few examples we see here of doing things we shouldn't.

> Ephesians 4:28-30 "Let him that stole steal no more: but rather let him labour, working with his hands the thing which is good, that he may have to

give to him that needeth. Let no corrupt communication proceed out of your mouth, but that which is good to the use of edifying, that it may minister grace unto the hearers. And grieve not the holy Spirit of God, whereby ye are sealed unto the day of redemption."

1. Greed – both stealing and not giving to those in need are motivated by greed – vs. 28
2. Evil speaking – corrupt communication would be talking in ways or about things that are sinful. – vs. 29
3. Disobedience to the Holy Spirit – When we are convicted and don't respond in obedience to the Holy Spirit we grieve Him. – vs. 30

I have made a comprehensive list below for you to follow as you read this passage. As you read through and follow this list circle the number by any access point that you have been involved with in the past. These are potential places that you have given a place for the devil to effect you. I encourage you to pray before you begin making your list and simply ask God to open your eyes and show you areas that you might have knowingly or unknowingly given the Devil access.

# Access Points according to Ephesians

1. Not walking worthy of my calling as a believer. – 4:1
2. Having pride – The opposite of lowliness and meekness – 4:2
3. Being impatient – The opposite of longsuffering and forbearing – 4:2
4. Not loving one another – 4:2, 5:2
5. Being contentious or causing strife – The opposite of unity and peace – 4:3
6. Doctrinal Error – 4:4-16
    a. Concerning salvation: By grace through faith alone and available to all people.
    b. Concerning God: One God who is all powerful, eternal, present and personal.
    c. Concerning Christ: Born of a virgin, lived a sinless life, died on the cross, buried and rose again and is now ascended into the heavens and seated on the right hand of the Father.
    d. Concerning Spiritual Authorities: God has ordained and set pastors and teachers over us for our growth and admonition.
    e. Concerning the Church: A local visible with a pastor and members started by Christ during His earthly ministry to carry out the great commission.
    f. Concerning Doctrine: Established by the word of God and always to be compared back to that. We are to beware of false teachers and false doctrines. We are to always speak the truth of God's Word in love.
    g. Concerning Unity: Comes from following Christ and being obedient to His Word.
7. Participation in the sinful parts of the world's culture – 4:17-19
    a. Vanity of the mind: Moral depravity
    b. Past feeling: A seared conscience because of repetition in sin
    c. Lasciviousness: Unbridled lust and shamelessness
    d. Uncleanness: Lustful living.
8. Not putting off the former conversations, the old man – 4:20-22
9. Not putting on the new man – 4:23-24
10. Lying – 4:25

11. Anger – 4:26-27, 31
12. Greed – Both stealing and not giving to those in need are motivated by greed – 4:28
13. Evil speaking – Corrupt communication would be talking in ways or about things that are sinful. – 4:29, 31
14. Disobedience to the Holy Spirit – When we are convicted and don't respond in obedience to the Holy Spirit, we grieve Him. – 4:30
15. Bitterness – 4:31: Holding a grudge.
16. Wrath – 4:31: Violent Anger or with a desire for vengeance.
17. Clamor – 4:31: Repeated loud outbursts of complaint.
18. Malice – 4:31: A desire to hurt another.
19. Being unkind – 4:32: Acting in a way to hurt the feelings of another.
20. Being hard-hearted – 4:32: Not considering the pain of others.
21. Unforgiveness – 4:32: Rejecting the sacrifice of Christ as sufficient to cover the offenses of others.
22. Not following the Lord – 5:1: Disobedience to the know will of God.
23. Fornication – 5:3: Sexual relationships outside of marriage.
24. Covetousness – 5:3: Lust, usually for possessions that belong to another.
25. Filthiness – 5:4: The use of obscenities.
26. Foolish talking – 5:4: Talking about sinful things
27. Jesting – 5:4: Telling dirty jokes
28. Not being thankful – 5:4
29. Whoremongering – 5:5: Engaging physically with whores.
30. Idolatry – 5:5: Putting anything or anyone above God in your attention and desire.
31. Taking part when others do these things – 5:6-7
32. Not walking in the light – 5:8
33. Not bearing the fruit of the Spirit – 5:9
34. Not proving what is acceptable to the Lord – 5:10: Knowing what is right but not doing it.
35. Having fellowship with the works of darkness (demonic activities) – 5:11
    a. Ouija boards
    b. Palm readers
    c. Horoscopes
    d. Tarot cards

  e. Seance
  f. Voodoo
  g. Satanism
  h. Spells
  i. Dungeons and Dragons or any games that include witchcraft.
  j. Witches or warlocks or things associated with them.
  k. Vampires, werewolves or other such demonic ideas.
  l. Or any other thing that is connected with the Occult.
36. Speaking about demonic activities – 5:12-13
37. Not being awake to Christ – 5:14-15
38. Wasting your time – 5:16
39. Not seeking the will of God – 5:17
40. Being intoxicated – 5:18
41. Not being filled with the Spirit – 5:18
42. Not having your heart set on the Lord – 5:19
43. Not being thankful – 5:20
44. Not being submissive to authorities or being involved in conflict – 5:21
45. Marital issues – 5:22-33
  a. Husbands not loving their wives as God commands
  b. Wives not reverencing and submitting to their husbands as God commands
46. Children not being obedient to their parents – 6:1-3
47. Parents not leading their children properly – 6:4
48. Provoking your children to wrath – 6:4
49. Employees not being obedient to their bosses – 6:5
50. Serving for man's approval rather than God's – 6:6-8
51. Bosses not leading their employees properly – 6:9

Fourteen

# *Closing the Access*

Now that you have made your list of potential access points from God's Word, it is time to close any that are open. It is not enough to know what the access points are, you actually need to do the work of closing them so that you remove the influence of the Devil in those areas. Take the following steps to work through this process.

1. Pray and ask God to open your understanding and memory to know if you have been involved in any of these areas.
2. Praying through each point on the list of access points, make a thorough list of each time the Lord reminds you of engaging in one of these things.
   a. Some points may have numerous events that you need to write down, some may not have any.
   b. Please remember, this is not just about what you remember. It is about asking God to show you where the problems are. That is why you need to pray over each access point and seek His help.
   c. Take your time.
   d. This list may be quite long and that is ok.
3. Once you have made your list, you will deal with each item on it in the following manner. <u>Do this out loud</u>, the Devil cannot read your mind; he can however hear your voice. You want him to know that you have turned to the Lord

in these areas and they are no longer available to him to exploit.
   a. Confess to God your involvement as sin
   b. Ask God to forgive you for that sin.
   c. Acknowledge to God that you have given place to the Devil in this area and that you are closing the access to the devil that you have given by your sin.
   d. Command any unclean spirits that are using this access to depart in the name of Jesus Christ.
   e. Ask God for healing and wisdom to prevent future involvement in that area.

Let me remind you that you are at this point fully engaged in spiritual warfare and you can expect to be attacked but your position in Christ is secure and you have a new identity in Him, a new purpose and because of this you can have boldness as you take these strong holds back from the Devil. With confidence in the power of Christ, go before the throne of God and remove the places that you have yielded in your past.

It may take you quite a while to work through this list. Be diligent to walk through each point and each step to renounce your involvement in these things. Be prepared for the Enemy to fight you as you do this; he will not willingly give up access that he has taken. Remember the instruction that we are given on this matter in 2 Corinthians and Revelation 12:11.

2 Corinthians 10:3-6 "For though we walk in the flesh, we do not war after the flesh: (For the weapons of our warfare are not carnal, but mighty through God to the pulling down of strong holds;) <u>Casting down</u> imaginations, and every high thing that exalteth itself against the knowledge of God, and bringing into <u>captivity</u> every thought to the <u>obedience of Christ</u>; And having in a readiness to revenge all disobedience, when your obedience is fulfilled."

If Satan tempts you to sin during this time, practice the 3 C's found in this passage.

Cast down – don't let your mind wonder, when some imagination comes into your mind reject it and refuse to consider it. It might be sinful behavior or even blasphemous thoughts against God, recognize that these are your enemy speaking and reject them.

Capture – grab hold of your thinking and refuse to let the Enemy draw you away from the battle that you have engaged in.

Correct – exercise your mind in obedience to Christ and revenge all the disobedience that the Wicked one has enticed you into.

Also remember what we have learned about the 3 P's

Revelation 12:7-11 "And there was war in heaven: Michael and his angels fought against the dragon; and the dragon fought and his angels, And prevailed not; neither was their place found any more in heaven. And the great dragon was cast out, that old serpent, called the Devil, and Satan, which deceiveth the whole world: he was cast out into the earth, and his angels were cast out with him. And I heard a loud voice saying in heaven, Now is come salvation, and strength, and the kingdom of our God, and the power of his Christ: for the accuser of our brethren is cast down, which accused them before our God day and night. And they overcame him by <u>the blood of the Lamb</u>, and by <u>the word of their testimony</u>; and <u>they loved not their lives unto the death</u>."

If Satan accuses you of your past to try and get you to stop claiming your present position and identity in Christ then practice the 3 P's found in this passage.

Plead the Blood – Since you are saved your past sin has been placed under the blood of Jesus Christ and God has forgiven it.

Praise the Lord – the word of our testimony is what God has done for us. Simply begin to praise the Lord out loud for all that He has done for you and then continue to praise Him for everything you can see or think of until the Devil withdraws from attacking you.

Practice the truth – they loved not their lives unto the death. Continue to do what you know God has called you to and finish closing the access points.

Since we are depending on God to show us where we have left access points open, we are also likely to find demonic influence present in those areas. Using the weapons of your warfare you will be able to cast out that influence and close that access. Just as with any access point though, If the door is open and no one is in the way, you can close it easily. If though, you go to close an access point and the evil one is using that entry then it will be more like trying to close a door someone is trying to push open, it will not be as easy in that situation, it will be full spiritual warfare. You are prepared to do this because you now know the truth about your position, identity and purpose in Christ and you can exercise the boldness that Christ has given you. Do not let an adversity in this effort stop you, push forward until you have finished your task.

# Fifteen

# *Maintaining Your Security*

Now that you have taken the steps needed to gain victory over the past, you need to learn how to maintain that victory. Of course, a big part of that is simply being watchful against opening the access points in your life again. But the book of Ephesians goes on to give you more details about the tactics of the Devil and the spiritual protection that God has given you through the armor of God. Your task is now to study through *"The Armor Plated Life"* volumes 1 & 2 to continue to grow into the warrior that God has called you to be. God has a great life of victory prepared for you and it is important for you to know how to prepare for what He has in store. Congratulations on finishing the first step in Spiritual Warfare, now strive to be like the Apostle Paul and be able to say…

> 2 Timothy 4:7-8 "I have fought a good fight, I have finished my course, I have kept the faith: Henceforth there is laid up for me a crown of righteousness, which the Lord, the righteous judge, shall give me at that day: and not to me only, but unto all them also that love his appearing."

I also encourage you to work through *"The Inner Man"* a study on the book of Philippians that will give you insight into how to control your mind and gain victory over your thinking.

# DO THYSELF NO HARM

Sixteen

# Thieves of Hope:
# Loss Control or Insecurity Issues

Not all people have positions of power over others, so you may not think this applies to you. However, all people have control over something, even if it is only over small decisions in their own lives. When this control seems to be slipping away, we can begin to allow our personal insecurities to dominate our thinking. This loss of control can push us to a dark place where hope is lost.

There are four times in the Bible that we see people who had power over others, only to have it taken from them. In each of these cases, these people committed suicide rather than giving up their control. These people were Abimelech in Judges 9:53-54, Samson in Judges 16:29-30, Saul in 1 Samuel 31:3-4, and Zimri in 1 Kings 16:18. These were quite unique situations as each of these men were facing capture by their enemies. In each of these situations, the men had lost hope that they could either escape or that they would be treated fairly. So instead of facing their enemies, they decided to kill themselves. All of these men were facing or had experienced a loss of position, power, and control. In many cases, the pursuit of power or control over others is a means to cope with insecurities in our own lives. While we might not often think about people who aspire to position and power as being insecure (since they often try very hard to portray a public face of confidence), insecurity is a problem that nearly everyone faces at some level. When we seek to compensate by controlling those around us and we lose that position or power it can leave us devastated and fearful.

While all of these men occupied a great position of power civilly, you don't have to be a king to experience this reality. Position, power, and control come in all shapes and sizes. Within the peer group of children, there is someone who feels that they have an elevated position, some level of power, and can control their peers. In reality, these factors can occur in any home, workplace, club, or organization. It doesn't take much power for it to go to some people's heads. The head of an H.O.A. might think that they have control over their neighbors. The manager of a company might try to exercise outsized power over their workgroup. A mayor or city council member might try to exert pressure or control over citizens in a way that is beyond the scope of their office. The adage is often correct, power corrupts. People often have a hard time reigning in their egos when they feel that they have some power over others.

As a result, when this power is lost they cannot stand the idea that others are equal to them or worse yet that others could have power over them. Their insecurities get the better of them and that is when the suicidal thoughts kick in. The real answer is not to kill yourself but to deal with your insecurities in the right way instead of the wrong way that you used before. To understand the Bible's answer to insecurity let's look at a passage of scripture.

> Psalm 142:1-7 "Maschil of David; A Prayer when he was in the cave. I cried unto the LORD with my voice; with my voice unto the LORD did I make my supplication. I poured out my complaint before him; I shewed before him my trouble. When my spirit was overwhelmed within me, then thou knewest my path. In the way wherein I walked have they privily laid a snare for me. I looked on my right hand, and beheld, but there was no man that would know me: refuge failed me; no man cared for my soul. I cried unto thee, O LORD: I said, Thou art my refuge and my portion in the land of the living. Attend unto my cry; for I am brought very low: deliver me from my persecutors; for they are stronger than I. Bring my soul out of prison,

that I may praise thy name: the righteous shall compass me about; for thou shalt deal bountifully with me."

The introduction to Psalm 142 says, "Machil of David; A prayer when he was in the cave". When David wrote this Psalm, it was a time of great insecurity in his life. The word insecurity simply means not feeling secure or safe. That feeling is expressed many times in the Psalms as David was running for his life from Saul. I suppose that you, like me, have never been on the run for your life, but take a moment and consider the reasons that David felt insecure during this time that we can identify with.

Sources of Insecurity:

Conflict: David was experiencing a great deal of conflict with Saul. He lived in Saul's house and ate at his table. David looked up to Saul as a mentor and father figure, but now there was nothing but conflict between them.

Separation from loved ones: David was already separated from his own family because of joining Saul's army; he couldn't go back to them for fear that Saul would kill his whole family. Now David was also separated from Saul, as well as from his friend Jonathan and his other companions. You read in Psalm 142 that no man would know him and that no man cared for his soul. This separation from his loved ones caused David to feel isolated, which was a great cause of insecurity for him.

Change: Everything that David had known was turned upside down. His home was gone, his job was gone, his friends were gone, and all he could do was run for his life. He says in the Psalm that refuge failed him; he had nowhere to go, so here he was sitting in a cave with nothing left.

Rejection: David certainly would have felt rejected by Saul, first because of Saul's anger at him, and secondly because Saul made it clear by his actions and words that he wanted to kill David. Not only this, but it had not been very long before that as David returned from battle, he heard people calling out that "Saul has slain his thousands and David his ten thousands." David was a national hero and now no one was willing to help him; he was rejected by everyone and alone.

Most people experience natural insecurity mostly between the ages of 7-16. It is during these ages that a course is generally set because of insecurity that causes many to grab hold of something to give them a feeling of security, and those things often become compulsive behaviors or addictions. The compulsion to control others or gain power and position can be just as strong as the compulsion to use any drug. The same issues that David faced are sources of insecurity for nearly everyone. Consider these reasons in a more personal application.

Conflict – This often comes in the form of fighting between parents. When parents fight, the children experience a great amount of insecurity. There is almost nothing more frightening to a young person than the prospect of losing one of their parents. Parents are a significant source of our security and when they are in open conflict, the fear increases in children.

Separation from loved ones – This can happen because of the death of a friend or a loved one. Losing someone close to you can turn your whole life over, regardless of your age. Many people have wrongly attached their own identity to that of another person and when the other person dies, they suddenly lose their source of personal identity and security. Divorce is another significant factor in this regard. When a parent, most often a father, is suddenly removed from the home because of divorce, it creates a tremendous amount of insecurity in a child. I have even known people whose parents divorced in their adult years. They were thrown into a significant amount of insecurity because the separation of their parents removed the foundation for their security. Divorce is an incredibly destructive and destabilizing event for children, regardless of their age. For a child, there is no such thing as an amicable divorce.

Change – aging provides its own insecurities as we grow and change. Moving from one class to another in school or moving to new schools as we grow can create feelings of insecurity. Add physical changes such as puberty and you increase insecurity even more. For many people, moving from place to place is a way of life, and such moves provide insecurity for a young person. They lose their friends and now are alone and must make new friends from strangers. New schools, new churches, new everything, all out of their control. There is a great desire to fit in that is a result of our insecurities, and so often when a person is plucked from the place that they are accustomed to and placed in a new environment, they experience peer pressure in a whole new way. They have no one and long to be accepted, so they will do things or change their behavior to be accepted because of the new insecurities that they are experiencing. Both separations from loved ones and change are the reasons that many missionary and military children struggle with insecurity and often fall prey to addictions as a result.

Rejection – This may be the result of anger in the home that is interpreted as a rejection of them as a person. It may be because of a parent or teacher who is a perfectionist and belittles them because of perceived weaknesses. It may also be the result of bullying or because of the rejection of peers that a person feels insecure about who they are, and as a result, begins to act out in a way to either gain acceptance or turns inwardly declaring that they don't need anyone else, that they can meet their own needs.

In all these cases, there is often a tendency to grasp for something that can relieve the feelings of insecurity that have resulted. It is during these vulnerable times that a trap is often laid and fallen into, a trap that provides a false feeling of security. David warns about that very thing in Psalm 142. He says in verse 3, "they privily laid a snare for me". In verses 6-7, he gives some other indications of what happens when a person falls into the snare of insecurity, saying that he was brought very low. Insecurity will bring a person to a very dark, very low place, desiring to be delivered from his persecutors. We might understand that when a person grabs onto false security, they will feel some solace in it, but they will also feel that they are being drawn into a darker place. David recognizes that such things are stronger than he was.

When we consider the things that a person might grab to provide a feeling of security, we must understand that these are generally very destructive substitutes. Alcohol, drugs, pornography, overeating, escape into fantasy through role-playing games, gangs, etc. Some even go to an extreme of being hyper-controlling, trying to control everyone around them, becoming something like a dictator when they get married and have children, or if they get some authority at work or church, become incredibly demanding. All these things can seem to provide a sense of security at first, but at length, they become our persecutors and are stronger than we are, and just as David expresses in verse 7, they become our prisons. They often become prisons because they are kept as secret sins hidden from everyone else. Our secrets will become our prisons. They are also prisons because of their addictive nature.

In doing a fair amount of Biblical Counseling, I have seen this pattern repeated over and again. Someone experiences a crisis in their home between the ages of 8-14, shortly after this they are exposed to something that provides a false sense of security, and they become addicted to it. Later in life, though they may want to be free, they cannot seem to get victory over it. Often this is because they are trying to deal with the actions without dealing with the source that caused them to seek a replacement for what they were missing.

Many are overcome by those very temptations and believe that giving in to them will provide the feeling of security that they are missing. The reality is that when you give in to the temptation to sin you are more vulnerable than you have ever been. The deception that you are safe becomes a lie that you allow to bind you because it seems to solve the issue that you are facing. All the while, it has just opened more issues than you can imagine.

The same is true if a person turns to alcohol, drugs, overeating, fantasy games, or any other compulsive behavior as a means of attaining a feeling of security. These behaviors all make a person more vulnerable. You are not more secure when you are drunk or high; you just think you are. In reality, you have become a danger to yourself and others. This includes the false sense of security that comes from controlling others. Because this control is so difficult to attain and keep it will be like standing on the side of a cliff always looking at the drop below. Trying to maintain control in our lives to prevent the insecure feelings from returning will wear a person out completely and produce unbelievable mental fatigue.

The longer that you are involved in these destructive behaviors, the more that the root of the issue becomes unclear. The issue becomes not only seeking security but also seeking the temporary pleasure that is offered. Most of the time, however, the compulsion is increased during times of high stress, when there is a conflict with your spouse when there is a major life change such as moving, job change, or a change in the family of another kind when there is a death of a loved one or a feeling of rejection that occurs. All of these things stir once again the desire for security and cause the person to be overwhelmed with the compulsion to act upon what they have become convinced restores the feeling of security that they are missing.

If security cannot be restored by these activities, how can it be dealt with? David gives us a three-part answer in Psalm 142. First, he says in verses 1-2, "I cried unto the LORD with my voice; with my voice unto the LORD did I make my supplication. I poured out my complaint before him; I shewed before him my trouble." Before a person can get victory over the control thinking, compulsive behaviors, and addictions that have come because of their insecurity, they must recognize this as the source of their problem. David said that he poured his complaint out before God and showed Him his trouble. If you are pursuing a sense of security outside of God, then acknowledging that and admitting to God where you went wrong is the only proper starting place to getting right.

Many people have come for counseling, and in doing so, had a root source of their problems pointed out by God, and once they saw it, they refused to deal with it. They want to be free from their addictions, but they don't want to deal with the reason that they are bound by their addictions. Often this is because it is hard, to be honest with yourself and others about your past, which may be seen as another sign of weakness and insecurity. When men come into our discipleship home, I tell them in our first counseling session that they will never get victory without first being willing to deal with whatever needs to be dealt with, and second, without being completely honest with God, me, and themselves about the real issues. I have spent countless hours counseling side issues to the point of great frustration because the underlying issues were still concealed, and one side issue would just be absorbed by another. Until you deal with the root of the problem, you are wasting your time trying to change the fruit.

The second thing that we see David do is acknowledging that the way he would deal with his insecurity does not work; only God's way works. Another way to say this is that you must realize the fallacy of false security. He says in verse 3, "When my spirit was overwhelmed within me, then thou knewest my path." Doing it your way is what got you into the snare that has you imprisoned. Doing it your way has kept you bound by the fake sources of security that have never genuinely fulfilled your needs. If you are overwhelmed, it is time to stop doing it your way and accept that God knows the path you need to take. Anything outside of His path is full of snares and traps that will just lead to more prisons.

If you are going to get victory over your control issues and compulsions, then you must start seeing the false security for what it is. Your wrong responses have not made you more secure; they have made you more vulnerable. You are not more secure because you control others; you are more vulnerable because of the fear of losing control. You are not more secure because of pornography; you are more vulnerable because of the secrets, you are more vulnerable because of the damaging effect on your thinking, and it is leading to a hindrance in other relationships. You are not more secure because of alcohol; you are more vulnerable because of it, and you are hurting yourself and others. The same is true for drugs and food and every other compulsion that we substitute to try and fill our void of security. You must begin to be honest about what these things are. They have never been a real solution to your problem, but have only compounded your problems. The feeling of security that you got from them was fake, a façade, there was never any there, there. Realizing this will help you discount the false narrative in your mind that you need this to feel normal or secure.

The third thing that we learn from David here is that a person must restructure their thinking. In verse 4 David says, "I looked on my right hand, and beheld, but there was no man that would know me:

refuge failed me; no man cared for my soul." It was the old thinking that leads to his insecurity, but in verse 5, David expresses a new way of thinking by saying, "I cried unto thee, O LORD: I said, Thou art my refuge and my portion in the land of the living." You see David's real refuge was in the LORD. Throughout the Psalms, we see this expressed as David calls God his rock, his deliverer, his strong tower, his fortress, his shield, his buckler, his safety, and his refuge. All of these are expressions of security that come from a proper understanding of who God is. You never needed those things to provide you security; you needed a right understanding of who God is to you as His child.

God wants you to run to Him when you feel insecure instead of to your cave of compulsive behavior. He wants you to find your security in your relationship with Him instead of the prison of your addiction. The compulsions are stronger than you, but He is stronger than them. the prison is stronger than you, but He is the one who sets prisoners free. Countless verses speak to God being our source of security. These verses speak of God being our strength, tower, rock, fortress, or any other symbols of security. Read them, memorize them and claim them because they were not just for David, God recorded them for you to restructure your thinking about who He is and to help you to be able to hold onto Him in times when insecurity seems to overwhelm you.

My prayer for you is to learn what David knew about the security that is available in God. He said it well in Psalm 61:1: To the chief Musician upon Neginah, A Psalm of David. "Hear my cry, O God; attend unto my prayer. From the end of the earth will I cry unto thee, when my heart is overwhelmed: lead me to the rock that is higher than I. For thou hast been a shelter for me, and a strong tower from the enemy. I will abide in thy tabernacle for ever: I will trust in the covert of thy wings. Selah." Only when you learn this will you have freedom from the insecurity that your compulsions are rooted in.

What things from this chapter do you need to implement in your life right now to begin to deal with this issue?

What is the first step that you will take now to start gaining victory?

Please share this with someone you know so that you have accountability to help you make these changes.

Seventeen

# *Thieves of Hope:*
# Lack of or Loss of Identity

Our identity is our view of ourselves. That view is molded by many factors beginning at a very young age. The home we grow up in plays a significant role in the development of our identity from the way that our parents are with one another to the way that they train us and even the words that they use when they speak to us. The friends that we have influenced our identity as well as our education and accomplishments. The many factors that contribute to our sense of being and worth are too many to count. The personal confidence that we have is linked to our strength of identity as well. If we have a very secure sense of identity and worth, we will naturally be more confident and conversely the less secure we are in our identity the less confidence we will have.

As we age our identity can change based upon our abilities and accomplishments. Many times, when men meet they will ask each other about their work or hobbies. A woman will ask the same or may ask about children as well. We tend to place a value on people for what they do. Socially a parent may imply to their children that a doctor or lawyer is of more value than a plumber or electrician by the way they encourage their children in educational pursuit. Truthfully what your need is at the moment will determine who is of more value at that time, if your toilet is clogged the best lawyer in the world is of little value to you compared to a good plumber. Yet we allow social stereotypes and public opinion to often increase or decrease our perception of who we are and what we are worth.

We see an example of this when the Bible records that Saul's armor-bearer committed suicide upon seeing Saul die in 1 Samuel 31:5. The Bible doesn't tell us his name, and that is part of the indication of the problem. This man didn't have his own identity; his identity was wrapped up in his relationship with King Saul. Many people have allowed their own identities to be lost in the pursuit of someone else. If something happens to the one they are following, such as death or rejection, because they do not have a secure idea of who they are as an individual, they lose hope, leaving them in a dangerous position. They may ask themselves, "Who am I without this other person?" Unfortunately, they may come to the mistaken idea, like Saul's armor-bearer, that they are no one, and because of that, they may attempt suicide.

We can all tend to find something or someone to attach our identity to and in that way, we are putting ourselves in danger. Some years ago, I was on a mission field with a group doing outreach when I came across a woman who was sitting on her front porch in her pajamas, weeping. I asked if there was anything that we could do to help her, and she shared with us that her father had passed away and she had been having trouble dealing with his loss. I offered to bring the missionary back later that day to visit with her and she was receptive to that idea. When we arrived, she was still in her pajamas and in her living room her father's picture was prominently displayed, his military uniform was laid out over the chair, his war medals were laid out all in such a way as to be readily seen and remembered.

I began by asking how long it had been since her father had passed and she shocked me when she said that he had passed more than two years prior. In all that time she had become completely immobilized by grief. As she began to share her story, we found out that her mother had passed when her father was away at war and he was wounded in battle. When he returned, she became his caretaker at a young age. All of her life she had been the caretaker for her father and now that he had passed away, she was left in an identity crisis. Her identity had always been related to her father but once he was gone there was no identity left for her as she saw it.

This was possibly much the same way that Saul's armor-bearer felt. His life was all centered around Saul and his job so when Saul died there was nothing left for him as he saw it. When our identity is in something that can end, such as abilities, jobs, or other people, their loss can leave us completely incapacitated. This identity crisis can be avoided however if we learn what God says about identity and put it into practice. You see, for you to have an unchanging identity, it must be anchored in someone who is unchanging, that someone is God. In the Bible, we find truths that can help us set our identity in God where we will never lose it again.

Our old self-image is often a result of three factors. First, it comes from what we do and how we perform. We think our life has meaning based on how good we are at what we do. Men ask each other, what do you do? We act as though we were a machine that has value only based upon its usefulness in a given task.

Second, we find identity in the acceptance and approval of others. Sometimes self-worth and identity are more based upon what others think of us than what we do, many people become willing to do almost anything for approval and acceptance from their parents or piers going to crazy extremes as approval junkies.

The third way that we claim identity is by our sinful behaviors. we define ourselves by what sins we have been involved in. I am an alcoholic, I am an addict, I am a homosexual or bisexual, or whatever other terms they have made up today. Satan wants people to claim a negative view of self that is predicated on their sinful behavior. Remember when Christ came into the country of the Gadarenes he was met by the man coming out of the tombs. When Jesus asked him what his name was, his response was "my name is Legion for we are many". What he was telling Jesus was his sinful condition, not his given name. This is what his identity had become because of his sinful choices and as a result, he had begun to identify himself to others in this way. The image of the old man is in opposition to what Christ tells us our identity is in Him once we have received Christ.

Take a few minutes to consider how you have established your own identity. Write down a few words that you would use to describe yourself.

_____        _____

_____        _____

_____        _____

These represent how you have described your identity up until now, but you do not have to continue to let these things be what define you. God offers us a new identity in Christ when we receive Him as our Savior. Look up and write out the verses below and learn what identity God wants to give you.

**In Christ I am loved.**

Galatians 2:20

_____

_____

_____

Ephesians 2:4

_____

_____

_____

Ephesians 5:2

_____

_____

_____

2 Thessalonians 2:16

_____

_____

_____

## DO THYSELF NO HARM

1 John 4:10-11

1 John 4:19

Revelation 1:5

**In Christ I am accepted.**

Psalm 139:13-17

Romans 15:7

Ephesians 1:6

## In Christ I am forgiven.

Romans 4:7

Ephesians 1:7

Ephesians 4:32

Colossians 1:14

Colossians 2:13

1 John 2:12

**In Christ I am a Child of God.**

John 1:12

Romans 8:14

Romans 8:16

Romans 8:17

Galatians 3:26

Galatians 4:6

**In Christ I am changed.**

2 Corinthians 3:18

_____

_____

_____

2 Corinthians 5:17

_____

_____

_____

Ephesians 2:10

_____

_____

_____

Ephesians 4:24

_____

_____

_____

Colossians 3:10

_____

_____

_____

**In Christ I am holy.**

Romans 6:22

_____

_____

_____

2 Corinthians 7:1

_____

_____

_____

Ephesians 4:24

_____

_____

_____

1 Thessalonians 3:13

1 Peter 1:15-16

**In Christ I am righteous.**

Romans 5:19

James 5:16

1 Peter 3:12

___

1 John 3:7

___

**In Christ I am victorious.**

Romans 8:37

___

1 Corinthians 15:57

1 John 5:4

**In Christ I am made perfect.**

John 17:23

Philippians 3:15

2 Timothy 3:16

2 Timothy 3:17

_____
_____
_____

Hebrews 13:20

_____
_____
_____

Hebrews 13:21

_____
_____
_____

**In Christ I am protected.**

Romans 8:38-39

_____
_____
_____
_____

**In Christ I am secure.**

1 Thessalonians 5:23

1 Peter 1:3

1 Peter 1:4

1 Peter 1:5

**In Christ I am free.**

Romans 6:18

Romans 6:22

Romans 8:2

2 Corinthians 3:17

**In Christ I have joy.**

Galatians 5:22

Colossians 1:10

Colossians 1:11

1 Peter 1:8

Jude 1:24

---
---
---

**In Christ I have peace.**

John 14:27

---
---
---

2 Thessalonians 3:16

---
---
---

Galatians 5:22

---
---
---

## In Christ I have hope.

Hebrews 6:19

___

1 Peter 1:3

___

1 Peter 3:15

___

1 John 3:3

**In Christ I have gifts.**

2 Corinthians 9:15

Ephesians 2:8

Ephesians 4:7

Ephesians 4:8

1 Peter 4:10

_____

_____

_____

If your identity is established in Christ then it will never change. Hebrews 13:8 says, "Jesus Christ the same yesterday, and to day, and for ever." Because Christ never changes our identity is secure in Him. To have your identity in Christ you must receive Him as your Savior. Putting your faith in Christ to forgive your sin and save you is where a relationship with God begins. There are a few things that you must know but there is nothing for you to do other than decide to trust Him.

What you must know.

1. **That you are a sinner:** "As it is written, There is none righteous, no, not one: There is none that understandeth, there is none that seeketh after God. They are all gone out of the way, they are together become unprofitable; there is none that doeth good, no, not one. Their throat is an open sepulchre; with their tongues they have used deceit; the poison of asps is under their lips: Whose mouth is full of cursing and bitterness: Their feet are swift to shed blood: Destruction and misery are in their ways: And the way of peace have they not known: There is no fear of God before their eyes. Now we know that what things soever the law saith, it saith to them who are under the law: that every mouth may be stopped, and all the world may become guilty before God. Therefore by the deeds of the law there shall no flesh be justified in his sight: for by the law is the knowledge of sin. But now the righteousness of God without the law is manifested, being witnessed by the law and the prophets; Even the righteousness of God which is by faith of Jesus Christ unto all and upon all them that believe: for there is no difference: For all have sinned, and

come short of the glory of God;" Romans 3:10-23

2. **That your sin has a penalty:** "Wherefore, as by one man sin entered into the world, and death by sin; and so death passed upon all men, for that all have sinned: (For until the law sin was in the world: but sin is not imputed when there is no law. Nevertheless death reigned from Adam to Moses, even over them that had not sinned after the similitude of Adam's transgression, who is the figure of him that was to come." Romans 5:12-14

3. **That Jesus died in your place to pay for your sin:** "For when we were yet without strength, in due time Christ died for the ungodly. For scarcely for a righteous man will one die: yet peradventure for a good man some would even dare to die. But God commendeth his love toward us, in that, while we were yet sinners, Christ died for us. Much more then, being now justified by his blood, we shall be saved from wrath through him. For if, when we were enemies, we were reconciled to God by the death of his Son, much more, being reconciled, we shall be saved by his life. And not only so, but we also joy in God through our Lord Jesus Christ, by whom we have now received the atonement." Romans 5:6-11

4. **That if you will accept His payment your sins will be forgiven:** "For the wages of sin is death; but the gift of God is eternal life through Jesus Christ our Lord." Romans 6:23 "But what saith it? The word is nigh thee, even in thy mouth, and in thy heart: that is, the word of faith, which we preach; That if thou shalt confess with thy mouth the Lord Jesus, and shalt believe in thine heart that God hath raised him from the dead, thou shalt be saved. For with the heart man believeth unto righteousness; and with the mouth confession is made unto salvation. For the scripture saith, Whosoever believeth on him shall not be ashamed. For there is no difference between the Jew and the Greek: for the same Lord over all is rich unto all that call upon him. For whosoever shall call upon the name of the Lord shall be saved." Romans 10:8-13

Once you receive Christ as your Savior, putting on your new identity is accomplished by coming to faith that what God says about you is true and what you feel about your past is forgiven. God offers you a new life and a new identity is you will receive it. Many before you have received the gift of new life in Christ and have found that the identity they had before was put away and they were made new. Changing our identity is something God can do in us if we are willing to yield ourselves to Him and accept His paths of life instead of our paths that lead to despair. What will you choose today? Simply bow your head and call upon the Lord, acknowledge to Him that you are a sinner, and let Him know that you believe Christ died for you and rose again.

If you have previously received Christ as your Savior and have not yet begun to claim the new identity that He offers you, you can change that today by coming to faith on His Word that you have written above.

# DO THYSELF NO HARM

Eighteen

# *Thieves of Hope:*
# Loss of a Sense of Purpose

In Ecclesiastes 2:17, Solomon, a man given great wisdom by God, came to the place that he said, "Therefore I hated life; because the work that is wrought under the sun is grievous unto me: for all is vanity and vexation of spirit." Solomon had everything that a person could possess, he could do anything he wanted and yet he hated life.

I have found that this same sentiment is often present in those who are suicidal. They just see no reason to go on, they hate life and there is nothing that they see that can change that. They have the same issue that Solomon had. Their perspective is directed at the wrong place. I want you to consider what Solomon reveals about himself as he leads up to this declaration that he hated life.

"I said in mine heart, Go to now, I will prove thee with mirth, therefore enjoy pleasure: and, behold, this also is vanity. I said of laughter, It is mad: and of mirth, What doeth it? I sought in mine heart to give myself unto wine, yet acquainting mine heart with wisdom; and to lay hold on folly, till I might see what was that good for the sons of men, which they should do under the heaven all the days of their life. I made me great works; I builded me houses; I planted me vineyards: I made me gardens and orchards, and I planted trees in them of all kind of fruits: I made me pools of water, to water therewith the wood that bringeth forth trees: I got me servants and maidens, and had servants born in my house; also I had great possessions of great and small cattle above all that were in Jerusalem before me: I gathered me also silver and gold, and the peculiar treasure of kings and of the provinces: I gat me men singers and women singers, and the delights of the sons of men, as musical instruments, and that of all sorts. So I was great, and increased more than all that were before me in Jerusalem: also my wisdom remained with me. And whatsoever mine eyes desired I kept not from them, I withheld not my heart from any joy; for my heart rejoiced in all my labour: and this was my portion of all my labour. Then I looked on all the works that my hands had wrought, and on the labour that I had laboured to do: and, behold, all was vanity and vexation of spirit, and there was no profit under the sun." Ecclesiastes 2:1-11

There is no doubt that Solomon did an amazing number of things. Many people have spent their whole life focused on just one of these things, and for the most part, these are good things, with only a few exceptions. So why with all his resources, wisdom and knowledge did Solomon come to hate life? The reason is not because of what he could or could not do, the reason lies in the language that he used to describe the achievements. In 11 verses of scripture Solomon uses a personal pronoun 44 times, an average of 4 times per verse. It wasn't what Solomon was doing that was the problem; it was who he was doing it for. When our sole purpose becomes about ourselves, we will become disenchanted with life itself. If there is no greater purpose than pleasing yourself, then life loses purpose all together.

It is important here not to confuse tasks with purpose. Each of the things in Solomon's list here are activities, tasks that he did. Tasks are how you fulfil a purpose, but they are smaller in nature. As you read the above passage, it is clear that Solomon's purpose had become to fulfill himself and he used these tasks to try and accomplish that.

In an earlier chapter you were encouraged to find a purpose verse that you could focus on for your life. I experienced the power of this in my life several years ago. In mid-1999, my wife and I were on the brink of divorce. Our lives and marriage were in major trouble. At the time I had been pastor of a church for several years, and yet at home we were in constant conflict. God graciously opened a door for us to come to Oklahoma City to begin studying Biblical counseling under Dr. Mike Hays. In one particular lesson on marriage counseling, Dr. Hays was emphasizing that the only Biblical reason to get married was if doing so would help you bring more glory to God than you could single. He was basing this on 1 Corinthians 10:31, "Whether therefore ye eat, or drink, or whatsoever ye do, do all to the glory of God."

That thought caught my attention. I began to wonder what the purpose of our marriage was. We had spent our entire marriage serving God. We had started two churches and been pastoring for 5 years at that point. In ministry endeavor we were certainly focused on bringing glory to God by what we did, but did that same purpose bleed over into our marriage? I began to talk to my wife about that thought and we came to the conclusion that we, in fact, had no unifying purpose in our marriage. We got married because we were "in love". We both wanted to serve God, but that had become what we did outside of our home and not the guiding purpose within the walls of our home.

I remember the day that we knelt down and committed our marriage to the purpose of bringing glory to God. No, it didn't change everything that was wrong in that very minute, but it did start us down the path of change that revolutionized our marriage. From that point on we began to evaluate the things that we did and decision we made in light of our new purpose. We began to make different decisions that we had before. We began to treat each other differently than we had before. I was impacted in one Sunday night service by Philippians 2:14, "Do all things without murmurings and disputings:" As I considered this in light of our purpose, I realized that fighting with my wife was preventing me from fulfilling our purpose of bringing glory to God. I repented and committed myself to walking according to God's direction.

Over 20 years later we have a happy and wonderful marriage. At the time, what seemed doom to failure and was a source of sorrow became a thing of perpetual joy in our lives. I know without a doubt that the change all stems back to that one decision to set a purpose for our marriage that was greater than simply being happy. You see, the purpose of life must be greater than self-fulfillment or some project. Projects end. If your purpose is simply a task, then when it is over you will become depressed. If your purpose is self-fulfillment you will become disenchanted because you will find just like Solomon that you are never satisfied with when you get what you thought you wanted. When you get everything you ever wanted there will still be a void because God didn't create things to fulfil us. He alone can fulfil us.

Solomon came to this realization himself when he said in Ecclesiastes 12:13 "Let us hear the conclusion of the whole matter: Fear God, and keep his commandments: for this is the whole duty of man." Solomon was saying that his focus on self-fulfillment was the problem. Purpose must transcend yourself and this life. Purpose must be greater than tasks. At some point everyone comes face to face with the end of their tasks. For some it happens earlier in life and for some it comes later. As a pastor I have known many pastors who as they reached the end of their pastoral ministry that struggled with whether their life was worthwhile any longer. I have sat with preachers who after a long and fruitful ministry told me that their life was now worthless. I have expressed to them my thoughts about all the lives that were changed by their ministries and the people who are now serving God because of their work, which was of little comfort to them. I have come to realize that what they are really saying is, "I don't have a purpose to live any more".

They had made the mistake of making their ministry their reason for living. I understand that because I was there myself at one point. I don't think this is exclusively a pastoral problem. I believe that most people confuse what they do with their purpose for life. It is likely that most people reading this right now are in the same situation. Your career cannot be your purpose, or you will lose it someday. Your children cannot be your purpose, nor can your marriage, hobby, entertainment, or anything else that is earthly focused. Purpose must transcend you and this physical existence. Of course, purpose affects what we do, it helps us define what to do in our life, but it is greater than the doing of these things.

I know that God has called me to be a pastor, but that is simply how I am fulfilling my greater purpose of bringing glory to Him. Some day He may change my task, but that won't change my purpose. It won't take away my reason for living because my purpose is not focused on the current task that He has given me. It is likely in our marriage that one of us will outlive the other, when that happens the purpose of bringing glory to God will still continue for the living. You see a purpose that transcends this life means that the reason for life always continues regardless of what changes we encounter.

If you identify with what I have been writing about here, then I encourage you to seek God for a greater purpose yourself. It doesn't have to be the same as mine, though you are welcome to use that. I recommend that you pray and ask God what purpose He wants in your life. Seek His Word and let Him give you a defining verse of scripture to base your purpose on. Make sure that your purpose is something that transcends tasks, people, or anything on this earth that has an ending point. Purpose must be God focused to endure. Once you have established your purpose write the verse below and give do an evaluation of how this will affect your tasks moving forward.

Purpose verse: _____

_____

_____

Simply state your new purpose: _____

_____

How does this purpose affect your tasks? _____

_____

_____

# DO THYSELF NO HARM

Nineteen

## *Thieves of Hope:*
# *Feeling Despised or Shamed*

Feelings of shame or being despised by others can come from many different sources. These feelings may arise from being misunderstood by others, from making a mistake, or from having a secret revealed. Sometimes, shame even comes from having our ideas rejected by others. The truth is that there are multitudes of situations that might cause us to feel despised or ashamed. Everyone feels these emotions at times. The problem often is when these feelings push against our pride and become magnified by our own mind. We can often think that others are thinking more about us than they actually are. Whether that is true or not, these feelings can be overwhelming to the mind if they are not brought into control.

There was a man with a strange name in the Old Testament of Ahithophel. He was a counselor to a man who wanted to be the king. Ahithophel's counsel was considered to be so good that is says in 2 Samuel 16:23, "And the counsel of Ahithophel, which he counseled in those days, was as if a man had enquired at the oracle of God: so was all the counsel of Ahithophel both with David and with Absalom." The word oracle means the very word, that is to say, as if they had heard from God Himself.

One day Ahithophel gave his counsel and the king decided to accept the advice of someone else instead. Ahithophel's pride was so wounded in 2 Samuel 17:23, that he left and killed himself. Sometimes, we let our pride become so large that we think we are being personally rejected when people don't accept our opinion. Proverbs 11:2 says, "When pride cometh, then cometh shame: but with the lowly is wisdom." We can take up offenses against others that lead to great bitterness or, such as in this man's case, lead us to consider death rather than being shamed in front of others. The feeling of shame is something that no one likes, but when it drives us to consider killing ourselves, it is an indication that our pride has gotten out of hand. The Bible tells us that Jesus despised the shame of the cross to redeem us. He knows how to deal with shame and reproach, and He can help you through this problem as well.

Shame is often associated with nakedness or the idea of being exposed in the Bible. Consider the following verses that demonstrate this.

> Genesis 2:25 "And they were both naked, the man and his wife, and were not ashamed."
>
> Exodus 32:25 "And when Moses saw that the people were naked; (for Aaron had made them naked unto their shame among their enemies:)"
>
> Isaiah 47:3 "Thy nakedness shall be uncovered, yea, thy shame shall be seen: I will take vengeance, and I will not meet thee as a man."

To feel ashamed then is to feel that something that you were trying to conceal has been exposed for everyone to see. Whether that thing was good or bad is somewhat irrelevant to the feeling, it could be either way. Many things could make us feel ashamed or exposed but we need not go through a list here. The truth is that when you feel that you have been shamed you know it already. Shame is a powerful feeling that can bring feelings of despair and suicidal thoughts as we have already seen. Often once we have experienced shame, we will live in fear of experiencing that again.

The question that we are going to deal with here is how to overcome the feeling of shame. Many verses in the Bible deal with shame and how to put it away. You may know some of these truths already but not applied them, some may be new to you, either way, I challenge you to meditate on these truths and apply them to your situation.

Believing in Christ removes the shame of sin because we know that our sins have been forgiven. This truth is given repeatedly in the Bible.

> Romans 9:33 "As it is written, Behold, I lay in Sion a stumblingstone and rock of offence: and whosoever believeth on him shall not be ashamed."
>
> Romans 10:11 "For the scripture saith, Whosoever believeth on him shall not be ashamed."
>
> 2 Timothy 1:12 "For the which cause I also suffer these things: nevertheless I am not ashamed: for I know whom I have believed, and am persuaded that he is able to keep that which I have committed unto him against that day."

When you receive Christ as your Savior the Bible teaches that your sins are forgiven by God for Christ's sake. No sin is left uncovered. Our shame and reproach are covered by the blood of Christ. God does not forgive us because we deserve it or we have earned it, it is all for Christ's sake alone. The Scripture teaches that Christ took our shame for us so that He could give us His righteousness. The nakedness of our sin is covered by His robe of righteousness. If you are going to get victory over shame it must begin with believing in Christ and receiving the righteousness that He offers you.

If you have trusted Christ as your Savior, the Bible gives us eight specific things that we can do to deal with shame in a direct way. As you consider each of these points please evaluate how you can apply them to your thinking and practice. Remember that our thinking process leads to how we feel. If we change how we think we will change how we feel. Don't let your feelings lead you, learn to think Biblically and you will feel differently than you do now. That reality leads us to our first step.

First, put your trust in God. I am not talking about salvation here, but rather trusting that God can overcome any obstacle you face. Repeatedly in the Psalms, David brings this thought out. Now David made some pretty big problems for himself. If you know your Bible, then you are aware that David committed adultery then had the woman's husband killed. He lied about the issue too before it was exposed. The truth is that David had much to be ashamed of, yet he constantly says that his trust in God overcame his shame.

> Psalm 25:2 "O my God, I trust in thee: let me not be ashamed, let not mine enemies triumph over me."
>
> Psalm 25:20 "O keep my soul, and deliver me: let me not be ashamed; for I put my trust in thee."
>
> Psalm 31:1 "To the chief Musician, A Psalm of David. In thee, O LORD, do I put my trust; let me never be ashamed: deliver me in thy righteousness."

Putting your trust in God doesn't mean that your sin won't be exposed, David's was. However, it does mean that you trust God to give you the strength to deal with whatever comes from it and to help you to overcome in spite of it. David still did great things for God and lead his nation after his sin was exposed. Sometimes having it exposed takes the greatest threat of it away, you cannot be fearful that it will be exposed once it has been. The greatest power sin has over us emotionally is that it will be known, once that is taken away and we have resorted to trusting God even though people know something terrible about us that thing has no more power over us to hurt us.

The second thing I see in the Scripture to put away shame is to pray. It says in Psalm 31:17 "Let me not be ashamed, O LORD; for I have called upon thee: let the wicked be ashamed, and let them be silent in the grave." Prayer is our outlet to God for pouring out our burdens. Often in the Bible, we see the prayer associated with the idea of cleansing or purifying. Our heart is cleaned when we pray and pour out to God our confession, sorrow, and burden. David, as we have said, committed many sins, but he also took them to God in prayer and poured them out before Him. This openness with God gave a cleansing to David from the burden of shame. Even if no one else knows, God knows all things. God sees all things and knows all things and we must realize that we cannot hide anything from Him. As such, prayer is not revealing anything to God that He doesn't already know. Prayer is however therapeutic to our soul as we pour out our deepest held secrets to our loving God who knows how to minister to us in the right way. The Holy Spirit is called the comforter for a reason.

The next several steps to dealing with shame are found in Psalms 119:78-80 "Let the proud be ashamed; for they dealt perversely with me without a cause: but I will meditate in thy precepts. Let those that fear thee turn unto me, and those that have known thy testimonies. Let my heart be sound in thy statutes; that I be not ashamed."

This passage shows us that the next step to dealing with shame is to put away pride. As we noticed earlier pride is a common source of shame. The opposite of pride is of course humility and you cannot put pride away without humbling yourself. Consider what it means then to humble yourself. Two things are important to understand to grasp humility. They are both present in one verse in 1 Peter 5:5 "Likewise, ye younger, submit yourselves unto the elder. Yea, all of you be subject one to another, and be clothed with humility: for God resisteth the proud, and giveth grace to the humble."

The first thing to notice is the idea of position or authority here. Notice that he talks about the younger and the elder this is a reference to the authority of either age or position. The first concept that it is important to understanding humility is to recognize that we as humans are neither the oldest nor the greatest compared to God Himself. That may seem a bit odd to say if you haven't ever thought about it, but God is from the beginning, He is by far the oldest, and He is the Creator which means He is also by far the greatest. Since humility recognizes a place of honor to those who are older and hold the greater position then all mankind should give such recognition to God as being their superior.

The second idea found in humility is that those who are superiors should be submitted to. A child should submit to the direction of their parents, why? They are superior in age and position, thus in authority. The word submit means to willingly put yourself under, this is humility, it is voluntarily putting yourself under the authority of another who because of their age, position, or authority is to be followed.

Let me draw that a bit farther. To put away pride means to recognize God as your superior and to submit yourself to Him. This doesn't even mean that you already agree with everything that He has said in His Word. You might not agree with everything in the Bible. I know that sounds odd, but it is true. Submission doesn't require agreement, it requires humility. It requires humility to accept that you don't know everything. It requires the humility to acknowledge that the way you have been doing it hasn't worked and that just maybe God has more knowledge than you. It requires that you acknowledge God as your superior and thus having the right to make the decision. It requires you to set aside what you think and do things God's way because He is your superior. Now, once you do things God's way, you will find that in fact, He does know what He is talking about and His way works. Humility must be put on first though to accept that even if you don't understand it, even if it doesn't make sense to you, He is still God and should be obeyed.

I also notice in Psalms 119:78-80 that we should meditate on God's Word. We will not understand everything but meditation on the Word of God will bring us to a greater understanding of God's way. Meditation is the meat of thought; it is not simply clearing your mind of all things. Meditation might be described as a cow chewing the cud. Cows have four compartments in their stomach, as they eat the unprocessed food goes into the first and then later is brought out to re-chew. This sounds a bit disgusting to us but it is how the cow can extract so much of the nutrition from what it eats. In other words, to meditate means to chew on it for a while, then chew on it some more. You will never understand the depths of meaning to a thing by a simple reading over it one time.

It says in Proverbs 18:13, "He that answereth a matter before he heareth it, it is folly and shame unto him." This is like saying, don't give an answer before you understand everything that relates to it. I think most of us have made that mistake before, giving an answer and later finding out that we didn't have all the facts. Well, meditation is like that with the Bible. God wants us to chew on it because it will take us a while to understand all the truth that is in it. The Bible is very truth rich and proper meditation is needed to process it all. The more we consume and process the truth into our heart, the more our mind is full of God's thinking and our wrong thinking is pushed out. The more that this happens the less shameful positions we will put ourselves in.

The final thing I notice in Proverbs 18:13 is that we are to give our heart completely to God's truth. Sometimes the problem is that we are mixing two or more things that dilute the truth. We live in a time when Post-Modernism is popular in the thought process. Post-Modernism says that you can hold two conflicting things as true at the same time. Such an idea causes people to make bad decisions because they are always simply using their emotions to decide which of the things they believe they will implement at the moment. The problem is that you will always implement the one that best serves you or your lust at that moment. The lack of absolutes becomes the basis for your destruction.

It cannot be that God is true and that something you believe contrary to the Bible is also true. Someone might say, well I believe most of the Bible, but I disagree about this point, whatever that might be. The problem is that you have just made yourself the arbitrator of truth. Either God is true or you are; you cannot both be true if you disagree. Putting away shame means you have to come to an agreement with God about what is true and only one of you can be right. Now let me assure you that it is God who is right. Romans 3:4 "God forbid: yea, let God be true, but every man a liar; as it is written, That thou mightest be justified in thy sayings, and mightest overcome when thou art judged."

Stop trying to correct God and accept that He is right. You have tried it your way and it hasn't worked, let's go back to humble yourself here and accept that His way is right. Stop questioning whether God is true and just believe Him by faith. Once you believe by faith you will begin to experience that He is true. That is the odd thing about Christianity. You don't see it until you believe it, and then you experience it and wonder how no one else sees it. Believe and you will see.

Steps six and seven for dealing with shame are found in Psalms 119:6-8 "Then shall I not be ashamed, when I have respect unto all thy commandments. I will praise thee with uprightness of heart, when I shall have learned thy righteous judgments. I will keep thy statutes: O forsake me not utterly."

First, we see here that we should obey God's commandments. It may sound very similar to the last point, but the difference is that you can believe something is true and still not do it. Here we are saying, do what God says. David reiterates this idea in Psalms 119:22-23 "Remove from me reproach and contempt; for I have kept thy testimonies. Princes also did sit and speak against me: but thy servant did meditate in thy statutes." Notice that reproach will be removed when I keep His testimonies, another way of saying do what God says in His Word. It says in James 1:22 "But be ye doers of the word, and not hearers only, deceiving your own selves." Many people will say they believe the Bible, but they are not doing what God says and they wonder why their faith isn't helping them. The reason is that they were deceived to think that saying you believe God without obeying Him would help them. It takes obedience to God's Word to receive the promise of God's Word.

I also notice that Psalms 119:6-8 tells us that we should praise the Lord. Often, we miss out on understanding just how important praise is to the heart. Praise to God is how we worship Him. Worshiping God is one of the primary needs of mankind. We were created with a need to worship. Many lost people fill this need by going to concerts and sporting events. Unfortunately, many believers fill their need there also. Worship changes us, it fulfills us as we pour out our adoration to God. It includes with it an outlet for humility. It is saying, "You are greater than I am, and I will acknowledge your greatness."

This attitude when poured out to other men it is idolatry, when poured out to God it is worship. Worship is the practical outlet of the proper expression of humility to God. To worship God says, He is greater than I am, so why am I so worried about what people think of me instead of what I think of Him. In a sense, worship is the abandonment of self-focus and a return of focus to where it should be. We are all sinners and in need of the Savior, to focus on my sin as greater than your sin is to be self-absorbed, rather we should both be worshiping the one who has forgiven us for our sin.

The final thing that the Bible teaches about dealing with shame is to wait on the Lord as it says in Psalm 25:3 "Yea, let none that wait on thee be ashamed: let them be ashamed which transgress without cause." Feelings follow decisions. When you make the right decision, you won't always feel good about it right away, but at length, your feelings change. A while back I was fat and tire. I didn't want to exercise and eat right. I decided to even though I didn't feel like it because it was the right thing to do. The more I exercised the decision against my feelings the more my feelings changed. Now I want to exercise, now I prefer to eat right because I have experienced how much better if feel.

When you start doing these things mentioned in this chapter you won't want to do them. They won't feel right, and you won't feel that they will work. Don't live on your feelings, live on God's truth. It won't change overnight, wait on the Lord. He will take away your feeling of shame as you exercise yourself to His truth that you have learned here. Keep doing what is right regardless of how you feel, and God will change how you feel.

What things from this chapter do you need to implement in your life right now to begin to deal with this issue?

What is the first step that you will take now to start gaining victory?

Please share this with someone you know so that you have accountability to help you make these changes.

# DO THYSELF NO HARM

Twenty

## *Thieves of Hope:*
# *Overcome with Guilt*

Guilt is a unique thing because it is both a fact-based proposition and a feeling that can be unrelated to the facts. In reality, someone is either guilty or not guilty but that often doesn't stop people who are innocent from feeling guilty. The issue that is at work here is the conscience. A person's conscience can either be sensitive so that they feel guilty at the slightest thing or hardened so that they don't feel guilty even when they have done horrible things. Our consideration in this section will address the issue of guilt from the idea that something was actually done wrong and the guilt is a result of that wrong doing. If this is not the case, then I recommend that you read the book *"Guilt: Dealing with an Accusing Conscience"* by this same author.

Probably the most commonly thought of incident of suicide in the Bible is that of Judas, who betrayed Jesus Christ. According to Acts 1:18-19, Judas killed himself in a field purchased with the money that he had received to betray Christ. There is no doubt that he was overcome with guilt and we could rightly say that he should have been. I cannot think of anything worse a person could do than to betray Jesus Christ. Some people carry so much guilt from bad decisions, and even criminal activity, that they are convinced this prevents them from receiving forgiveness and peace. This was the case for Judas, but he was just as wrong as they are. It may be that you are carrying guilt from past choices. I have good news: the Bible says Christ died for all our sins and you can find forgiveness and freedom from guilt by believing in Him. To find out how to get freedom from the guilt of your past, continue to read on.

One account of scripture that always comes to my mind when I think about feeling guilty is that of Joseph and his brothers. If you're not familiar with the account, Joseph's brothers were envious of him because their father favored him over all of them. They conspired to get rid of him and they did by faking his death and selling him into slavery. As time passed however Joseph ended up rising to the second in authority in Egypt. Shortly after that happened there was a great famine and Joseph's brothers were sent to get grain from Egypt and were brought before Joseph.

Now, this was awkward, here he was in authority and they were begging for help. The thing was, they didn't recognize him. He was dressed as an Egyptian would dress and who would have thought that this brother who was sold as a slave would be a man of great authority in Egypt. Joseph made it hard on them and something very telling happened. As they were there, they began to talk to one another in front of him, in Genesis 42:21 "And they said one to another, We are verily guilty concerning our brother, in that we saw the anguish of his soul, when he besought us, and we would not hear; therefore is this distress come upon us."

How interesting, they didn't know this was Joseph but when they were in trouble, they still felt guilty about what they had done all those years before. Guilt has a way of hanging around. It isn't often dulled by time and distance. It also tends to raise its head when bad things happen because we know that we are reaping what we have sown in some way. Joseph's brothers sure felt that they were reaping the consequence of what they had done. It says in Proverbs 28:1 "The wicked flee when no man pursueth: but the righteous are bold as a lion." People who have done wrong feel guilty and always think someone is after them, even if there isn't anyone coming for them at all. That is their conscience. God placed it in us to convict us of our wrongdoing and motivate us to make it right.

The good news is that God not only put that in us, He also made a way for us to overcome guilt. The way to overcome guilt is not complicated. There are just three steps to getting over guilt. I didn't say it was easy mind you. It isn't easy because to do this you will have to humble yourself at the very beginning. The weight of guilt that you have been carrying is far heavier than you imagine and laying it aside will lift the burden but many times our pride keeps us from doing what we must.

The first step to overcoming guilt is to confess your wrongdoing. Leviticus 5:5, "And it shall be, when he shall be guilty in one of these things, that he shall confess that he hath sinned in that thing:" In the Old Testament, the law of God is given in detail. There are 613 commandments in the Old Testament. The Bible tells us that the law was never intended by God however as a means for men to show that they were righteous. On the contrary, the law was intended to show us that we were not righteous. That truth is revealed to us in the New Testament in Romans 3:19, "Now we know that what things soever the law saith, it saith to them who are under the law: that every mouth may be stopped, and all the world may become guilty before God."

God knew that we would never be able to keep the law, and for those who think that they did pretty well because they kept most of it. He said in James 2:10 "For whosoever shall keep the whole law, and yet offend in one point, he is guilty of all." You see, keeping the whole law is not possible since we are sinners by birth. The law was simply a standard set to show us that we are sinners lest we begin to think that we are righteous without God. In the Old Testament, there was no supposition that someone would never break the law, instead, there were steps given for that person to be forgiven when they did. This same truth is present in the New Testament. The first step to redemption once you have sinned is to confess that you have sinned. This is a humbling experience. This is the point that Joseph's brothers came to the point that they knew they had done wrong, but they finally confessed it when the consequences got bigger than they expected.

Unfortunately, far too often we will justify ourselves until the consequences are overwhelming. That is the place that we have come to when we are considering suicide to escape the guilt. The overwhelming nature of our guilt has caused us that it would be easier to kill ourselves than live with it, but that is a deception. The right answer is not suicide, the right answer is confession. As long as we are alive, we can still do something to make a wrong thing right. Don't listen to the lie that it is too late. It is not, humble yourself and confess the wrong to God and others as needed. Doing this removes the guilt. confession cleanses the soul.

Confession is not the end of the process in the Bible, it is the first step though. The next thing that we must do is have a sacrifice to atone for the wrong. Leviticus 5:17-18 talks about this in the context of the Old Testament. "And if a soul sin, and commit any of these things which are forbidden to be done by the commandments of the LORD; though he wist it not, yet is he guilty, and shall bear his iniquity. And he shall bring a ram without blemish out of the flock, with thy estimation, for a trespass offering, unto the priest: and the priest shall make an atonement for him concerning his ignorance wherein he erred and wist it not, and it shall be forgiven him."

Now in the Old Testament, the sacrifices they brought were animals whose blood would be shed as atonement for their sin. The New Testament however tells us of the perfect sacrifice that was made to cover the sin of all mankind.

> Hebrews 9:11-14 "But Christ being come an high priest of good things to come, by a greater and more perfect tabernacle, not made with hands, that is to say, not of this building; Neither by the blood of goats and calves, but by his own blood he entered in once into the holy place, having obtained eternal redemption for us. For if the blood of bulls and of goats, and the ashes of an heifer sprinkling the unclean, sanctifieth to the purifying of the flesh: How much more shall the blood of Christ, who through the eternal Spirit offered himself without spot to God, purge your conscience from dead works to serve the living God?"

Jesus made the sacrifice for our sin on the cross. He shed His blood to pay the price for sin and according to Ephesians 4:32, God forgives us for Christ's sake. You don't need to make some personal sacrifice to atone for your wrongdoing, you do need however to accept that sacrifice that Christ made for you. You must accept that

Christ's death was for your sin and put your faith in Him for forgiveness. Our forgiveness is based upon what Christ has done and not what we can do. His death was sufficient to pay for all sin because God deemed it to be worthy. Jesus was God in the flesh who gave His own physical life as a redemptive sacrifice for us because the wages of sin is death. He gave His sinless life for our sinful one. Once we accept Him as our Savior, God credits His righteousness to us which covers our sin. When sin is covered there is no need to feel guilty.

Implied in the idea of confession and accepting the sacrifice of Christ is the understanding of repentance. Repentance is when a person turns from their old way of thinking to a new one. The old way of thinking may have said that what I did was justified, but my guilty feeling over it proves that wrong. The old way of thinking may have said there is nothing that can make it right but Christ's sacrifice and promise in the Bible to forgive proves that wrong. Repentance is turning from what you have believed (that there was no way to deal with the guilt), to acceptance of what God has said (that Jesus Christ's death, burial, and resurrection as sufficient payment for your sin).

The final step in dealing with guilt is the issue of restoration. Now restoration is not necessary for God's forgiveness, God forgives us because of Christ and not because of our works. But the Bible teaches that when we have truly repented of wrongdoing we will seek to make right what we can to those we have wronged. Not for forgiveness but because it is right. It says in Leviticus 6:4 "Then it shall be, because he hath sinned, and is guilty, that he shall restore that which he took violently away, or the thing which he hath deceitfully gotten, or that which was delivered him to keep, or the lost thing which he found,"

In Numbers 5:6-7 it says, "Speak unto the children of Israel, When a man or woman shall commit any sin that men commit, to do a trespass against the LORD, and that person be guilty; Then they shall confess their sin which they have done: and he shall recompense his trespass with the principal thereof, and add unto it the fifth part thereof, and give it unto him against whom he hath trespassed."

Probably the greatest example of this is found in the New Testament account of Zacchaeus. This is given in Luke 19:5-10 "And when Jesus came to the place, he looked up, and saw him, and said unto him, Zacchaeus, make haste, and come down; for to day I must abide at thy house. And he made haste, and came down, and received him joyfully. And when they saw it, they all murmured, saying, That he was gone to be guest with a man that is a sinner. And Zacchaeus stood, and said unto the Lord; Behold, Lord, the half of my goods I give to the poor; and if I have taken any thing from any man by false accusation, I restore him fourfold. And Jesus said unto him, This day is salvation come to this house, forsomuch as he also is a son of Abraham. For the Son of man is come to seek and to save that which was lost."

Zacchaeus made a living as a tax collector, but he had not been honest. Once he turned to Christ, he made his declaration that he would make restitution to those he had wronged. This had nothing to do with making him a believer, it was because he becomes a believer. Both the Old and New Testament teach us the power of restoration to healing the wounds of guilt. You don't need to sit around and try to remember everything you have done wrong, but that thing that you have been guilty over you should seek to make restitution in. It may not be completely possible, but you should try it. Making restitution takes away any residual guilt that you may still have.

Think about it like this. If you have stolen a car, you can go to God and confess it as wrong and even turn yourself in to the authorities and pay for the crime in jail. However, if you were truly retentive you would also give the car back. Trying to keep the car since you paid for your crime would be saying that you deserved the car for some reason. Of course, restoring the car to the owner is the right thing to do in addition to paying the price for your wrongdoing.

Now I don't know what it is that you feel guilt over, but I do know that the answer is the same regardless of the sin. Confess the wrong to God and the offended party, believe in Christ, and confess Him to receive forgiveness of your sin, and then make restitution of what you can to the one you have wronged. These three steps will give you victory over guilt.

What things from this chapter do you need to implement in your life right now to begin to deal with this issue?

What is the first step that you will take now to start gaining victory?

Please share this with someone you know so that you have accountability to help you make these changes.

DO THYSELF NO HARM

Twenty-one

# Thieves of Hope:
# *Feelings of Failure or Blinded by the Darkness*

Great men have often struggled with a feeling of creeping darkness. It is said that Winston Churchill did as well. Churchill gave it a name, he called it his "black dog". It is even noted in his journals and letters that he would avoid standing too close to balcony's and train platforms lest he was overtaken with a desire to end his life because of this. While there is some debate as to whether he struggled with some emotional issue, there is little doubt that the metaphor of being accompanied by a "black dog" resonates with many people when they feel impending darkness upon them.

Life is full of success and failure for everyone. Some seem able to brush off the failures and focus on the success more readily while others become overwhelmed by the failures and find it difficult to move forward even though others may see them as successful. There is an account in the Bible that seems to illustrate this quite well and it is found in Acts 16:25-31 "And at midnight Paul and Silas prayed, and sang praises unto God: and the prisoners heard them. And suddenly there was a great earthquake, so that the foundations of the prison were shaken: and immediately all the doors were opened, and every one's bands were loosed. And the keeper of the prison awaking out of his sleep, and seeing the prison doors open, he drew out his sword, and would have killed himself, supposing that the prisoners had been fled. But Paul cried with a loud voice, saying, Do thyself no harm: for we are all here. Then he called for a light, and sprang in, and came trembling, and fell down before Paul and Silas, And brought them out, and said, Sirs, what must I do to be saved? And they said, Believe on the Lord Jesus Christ, and thou shalt be saved, and thy house."

We don't know much about the jailer here at Philippi. He was at least moderately successful to have achieved this position, he had a family and what possibly an important position in the community. It would seem that he was at least a normal man with a career. But one night a tragedy befell him. There was an unexpected event, and an earthquake shook the jail. We all experience tragedy at some point in our life, some more than others but no one escapes without some.

Often when tragedy strikes, much like it did here it breaks up the foundations that things were established on. In this situation, there were two foundations shaken. The physical one that the jail was securely set on and the emotional one that the life of the jailer was set on. Every time tragedy strikes it is like an earthquake that hits our foundation. A strong foundation will withstand, though there may be some damage it will not destroy us, if we are rocked again and again it can eventually break up even the strongest emotional support.

When this happens the doors that we had locked tightly often spring open. Just as this jail did our emotional security becomes broken down. It may be things we have locked away for many years get set loose in our minds and we don't know what to do about it. Things that were bound up get lose and it can create a very fearful time in our hearts. I want to be clear that the biggest issue that we face during this time is our fear. It will seem that it is everything around us, but it is simply what is inside of us.

This Jailer experienced a tragedy that took away his inner security because the outer structure that he was depending on fell apart. In the darkness, he only saw what he feared. He presumed the worst, why didn't he call for a light first? It was midnight, so it was very dark. Many times, when people consider suicide, they describe the way that they feel as being dark. I know that this is talking about the night time, but I think there is a metaphor here that is interesting.

Darkness does something to us. It can bring confusion and it can bring fear. This man could not see clearly, and so he imagined the worst. That is what people do in the dark. The Bible says that he supposed the prisoners escaped and because of this wrong supposition, he was going to kill himself. He didn't even wait to examine and see if he was correct. Often in the darkness, we will jump to the conclusion that there is no hope without knowing the truth. We allow the darkness to create despair in our hearts and prevent us from finding out the whole truth.

He lost hope because of his fear in the darkness. The situation was totally out of his control and he could not see a way out. His only thought was that the worst thing he could imagine had happened. All the prisoners would have escaped. This was a serious thing for him since it could mean that he would be held responsible and be severely punished. He counted this as a personal failure. Now, we might all look at this situation and say, "there was nothing he could do, it wasn't his fault". We would be right, but he couldn't see that at the time. Just as you might be reading this and being in the darkness yourself you might think that the worst has happened and nothing can be done to fix it. The darkness that is surrounding you has you confused. The "black dog" is barking and seems to drown out everything else.

Something interesting happens here though in the Bible. Someone calls out to him. I find it interesting that the jailer couldn't see anyone, but someone could see him. Please listen to me right now, someone sees you. They may be a family member or a friend, but they see you, they may have given you this book and are concerned because you seem to be in the darkness without any hope. They know there is hope, they have probably tried to convince you of that, but you don't believe them. Please listen to their voice, they see you even if you cannot see through the darkness.

Paul had a two-part message for the jailer, a message that others have been trying to get to you. First, he said do thyself no harm. Don't react by doing something that will hurt you and others. It is dark where you are, but it isn't over for you. There is still light out there, there is still hope available. Do thyself no harm, don't follow through on your plans to end things. Hit the pause button there, there are some things that you don't yet know. You might suppose the worst but there are too many things that you still don't know.

The second message Paul had was that they were all there. What the jailer supposed was not true. There was no escape, there was no reason to harm himself even though in the darkness he couldn't see the truth. As I write this we are in November 2020, this is a pretty uncertain time. Sickness, politics, and economic uncertainty are all around and there are many things that we don't know. We are told that it will be a dark winter by some national leaders, and many people feel that darkness. Suicide rates have risen dramatically this year because of the darkness. But with all of that, we are still here. Your family is still here, your friends are still here and even more than that God is still here and He is waiting for you. You might not see it right now but there is hope, and those voices calling out to you in your darkness prove it, don't shut them out.

What happens next is important, the jailer heard the voice of Paul and he believed him. It was then that he (the jailor) called for a light. This seems odd to some, why wouldn't he have called for a light first? Why would he have presumed the worst instead of checking first? The darkness deceives us sometimes but never forget this; the light was available to him the whole time. There were always people nearby that were ready to give him the light when he called for it. The key here is that he had to decide he wanted the light. People might tell you there is light all the time but until you decide to call for it yourself it will still be dark. You have to decide to come back to the light.

The light reveals the truth. The truth that what he feared had not happened and that what happened did not destroy him. The truth that others cared about him. Imagine this, here is a man who is keeping a jail, and the prisoners inside care more for his life at that moment than he did. What a crazy thought, others who you might not even know care about your life. This goes against what we often believe in the darkness. The darkness says no one cares, others will be better off if I was not here and so on but this is all the lies of the darkness. The truth is revealed by the light.

Ultimately the biggest thing about the light is that you need to call on the true light. That true light is Jesus. My mentor in counseling told me about a counseling session that he had once with a woman who had fallen into prostitution and drugs. She told him that her life was a wreck and she just wanted to end it. He shocked me when he said that he told her he agreed. He said she was right, the life she had made was terrible but that if she wanted out of it, she didn't need to kill herself, she needed to get a new life. Jesus offers that new life; He offers a light that is brighter than the sun.

John spoke a lot about Christ being the light. Listen to what he says in John 1:1-9 "In the beginning was the Word, and the Word was with God, and the Word was God. The same was in the beginning with God. All things were made by him; and without him was not any thing made that was made. In him was life; and the life was the light of men. And the light shineth in darkness; and the darkness comprehended it not. There was a man sent from God, whose name was John. The same came for a witness, to bear witness of the Light, that all men through him might believe. He was not that Light, but was sent to bear witness of that Light. That was the true Light, which lighteth every man that cometh into the world."

Christ is the light that can take away your darkness. Jesus said of Himself in John 8:12 "Then spake Jesus again unto them, saying, I am the light of the world: he that followeth me shall not walk in darkness, but shall have the light of life." And then again John 12:46 He said, "I am come a light into the world, that whosoever believeth on me should not abide in darkness." If you have never believed on Christ, the way to receive the light is to put your faith in Christ and be saved today. If you have believed and you are struggling with the feeling of darkness it is likely because you are not in fellowship with the Light (Christ). Once you have received Him you are called to walk in Him.

You cannot say that you are walking in the light and darkness at the same time, the Bible specifically says that in 1 John 1:5-7 "This then is the message which we have heard of him, and declare unto you, that God is light, and in him is no darkness at all. If we say that we have fellowship with him, and walk in darkness, we lie, and do not the truth: But if we walk in the light, as he is in the light, we have fellowship one with another, and the blood of Jesus Christ his Son cleanseth us from all sin."

Can you hear my voice? Can you hear the voice of your family and friends? We're calling to you in the darkness. We know you don't see the light right now, but it is here and we are here, call for the light, come into the light and you will see that what you feel in the darkness isn't the truth. No matter how afraid you are right now, there is help and there is hope if you will come into the light again.

What things from this chapter do you need to implement in your life right now to begin to deal with this issue?

What is the first step that you will take now to start gaining victory?

Please share this with someone you know so that you have accountability to help you make these changes.

Twenty-two

# *Thieves of Hope:* ***Prolonged Sickness and Trials***

The Centers for Disease Control says that as of 2012 nearly half of all adults in America (117 million people) had some form of chronic disease. The likely hood is that you or someone you know suffers from chronic illness or pain. The results of this can be devastating both on the individual as well as the family. The consequences of such a situation are not only the financial cost but the emotional and spiritual burden that such a problem brings as well. These are the issues that are often the most overlooked, unfortunately.

No one in the world has had more sickness and trial than a man in the Bible named Job. In just a short time, he lost everything he owned, all his children died, and he got painful boils from the top of his head to his feet. His life went downhill fast and he was completely miserable, both emotionally and physically. It is no wonder why, in Job 6:8-11, he wished that he would die. Nothing can steal hope as fast as grief and sickness. Part of this is because we can forget that even in these things, we still have a purpose. We can lose sight of that purpose easily when with the distraction of physical and emotional pain. Job did this very thing, but by the end of the book of Job not only had he recovered from his sickness, but he had recovered all of the possessions he had lost and more. Without a doubt, Job had much to be sad about, but the Bible shows us that he didn't know the end of his own story. And neither do any of us. In the end, Job had far more good waiting for him than the bad he experienced. The Bible tells us that God can give us peace even while we face trials in life; this begins with having a personal relationship with Jesus Christ. To learn how to have that peace continue to read on.

I want to address the emotional and spiritual condition of those who struggle with chronic problems and try to give both insight and answers for the trial. Let's begin with the emotional side of things. People who have chronic illness and pain struggle with a variety of emotional issues. Anxiety over the illness itself, over the expenses, over the strain on their families, and over the prospects of ever having relief or recovery from the illness or pain can dominate the mind. Grief over the loss of personal abilities, health, family response, and social life can be overwhelming. Then there are the emotional issues of loneliness, depression, and the constant mental battle that you cannot take any more. These issues can be many times as devastating as the problem itself.

Can there be the hope of victory over the emotional problems even if the physical issues remain? The answer to that is yes, but not without a fervent dedication to the solution. Many times in counseling I have told people one of the most basic truths of life which is that life is not about what happens to you, it is about how you respond to it. Victory in life is not about what your circumstances are, it is about how you respond to those circumstances and whether you let them dominate you, or you rise above them. This is at its core a matter of cultivating a determined mind. The control of your mind is where you must begin if you are going to have victory over the emotional issues brought about by your situation. The Bible consistently teaches us that the main way to have victory over troubling thoughts is to develop directed thinking.

It says in Proverbs 23:7 "For as he thinketh in his heart, so is he:" If a person will develop control in their thinking they can have victory over their emotional life. There are two passages of scripture that give us some clear direction on how to gain this control over the thought life. The first of these passages is in 2 Corinthians 10:4-6 "(For the weapons of our warfare are not carnal, but mighty through God to the pulling down of strong holds;) Casting down imaginations, and every high thing that exalteth itself against the knowledge of God, and bringing into captivity every thought to the obedience of Christ; And having in a readiness to revenge all disobedience, when your obedience is fulfilled." You do not have to allow the strongholds of anxiety, grief, loneliness, depression, or other emotional responses to have a place in your mind. You can have victory over them by following the three-step process found in this text. First, cast down the wrong imaginations that you have been entertaining. Don't let your mind run wild into all the possible scenarios that could take place or into the poor me's. Determine not to dwell in negative thinking so that you don't make your bad situation worse with emotional problems. Casting down wrong imaginations means that you refuse to entertain the thinking about the negative side of your problems.

The second step shown here is to capture your thinking. It says "bringing into captivity every thought". Captured thinking means that you not only reject the negative thoughts but you purposely determine what you are going to think about. I will give you some tools to accomplish this in just a moment, but I want to lay the foundation here that directed thinking will help you to avoid the situation where your mind constantly runs to the negative. Captured thinking says, I will decide what my mind will dwell on, I will decide where my thoughts are directed. You cannot control the illness, you cannot control the pain but you can control your mind and when you have control over your mind you restore a central element that chronic issues rob people of which is the feeling of having control in their life.

The third step in 2 Corinthians 10 is to correct wrong thinking. It uses the phrase, "having a readiness to revenge all disobedience", this means that some of the wrong thinking that you have allowed may have embedded itself in your natural responses. You will have to root out any negative natural responses and reject them for the right biblical responses that you are going to put in their place. Often we don't realize just how much of our thinking and reaction is based upon our past thoughts and wrong beliefs. You will want to search out those wrong beliefs and replace them with the right ones so that you will not fall back into the trap of negative thinking.

The process of developing right thinking is explained in Philippians

4:4-9  "Rejoice in the Lord alway: and again I say, Rejoice. Let your moderation be known unto all men. The Lord is at hand. Be careful for nothing; but in every thing by prayer and supplication with thanksgiving let your requests be made known unto God. And the peace of God, which passeth all understanding, shall keep your hearts and minds through Christ Jesus. Finally, brethren, whatsoever things are true, whatsoever things are honest, whatsoever things are just, whatsoever things are pure, whatsoever things are lovely, whatsoever things are of good report; if there be any virtue, and if there be any praise, think on these things. Those things, which ye have both learned, and received, and heard, and seen in me, do: and the God of peace shall be with you."

Four points need to be understood from this passage to develop the right thinking patterns. The first step is to instill a spirit of rejoicing in your life. It says in Isaiah 61:3 to "put on the garment of praise for the spirit of heaviness". The way to develop the positive thinking of praise in your life is through having set times through the day to consider things that you can praise God for. I recommend that you keep a 3x5 card file and on one of these cards write three things that you can thank God for each morning, noon and evening. Doing this three times each day will give you a directed pattern of praise. Of course, at first, it may be hard to think of three things that you can thank God for because you have developed negative thinking patterns but the more that you practice this the more you will find that it lifts the veil of dark emotions that have tried to overcome you.

The second step in changing your thinking is to purpose moderation in your life. It is easy when one area of your life is out of control to allow other areas to follow suit. The scriptures said "let your moderation be known", this means that what areas you can control you should. I don't mean what people, I mean you can control some aspects of your daily routine, you can control your medications by not abusing them, you can control your diet, television viewing, social media posting, and many other aspects of your life. Don't allow one area that is beyond your control allows the rest of your life to become uncontrolled as well. Realizing that you still have a lot of control in life will help you direct your thinking to where it should be.

The third step in changing your thinking is to develop a real personal relationship with God. This itself is key in gaining control over the spiritual aspects of dealing with chronic problems. To have a real relationship with God you first must know Jesus Christ as your personal Saviour. If you don't know Christ as your Saviour I encourage you to learn more about how you can through the Bible studies offered here. If you do know Christ as your Saviour you must develop a close and intimate fellowship with Him through personal devotions. I encourage you to keep a devotional journal and make a record of your devotional time each day. Put the date in the top right corner so that you can be honest about your consistency. Write the passage that you are reading on the top left and in the first couple of lines write notes about your prayer time that day.

I use the Lord's model prayer as a template for my prayer time, which gives me five sections for prayer. First I spend time praising God for what He has done in my life and for who He is. I then spend time asking Him what He wants me to do for Him today, I ask who He wants me to minister to or witness to. It is important to ask God to help you minister to others, remember that as bad as things may be for you others have needs as well. After this, I ask God to meet my personal needs and I ask if there is anything that He wants me to ask for. The fourth part of my prayer is to ask forgiveness for my sins and also to ask God if there is anyone I need to forgive. Sometimes harboring unforgiveness toward others is a greater burden to carry than physical illness. Finally, I spend time praying for the needs of others.

After you pray, read the Bible and write down what God spoke to you about as you read. Every day God has a personal message for you from His Word. This message may be in the form of a promise that He has made, it could be a principle that helps you to make decisions in your life or it could be a commandment that God wants you to keep. Write down what stands out to you in the passage and how you can apply it to your life. If your chronic issues keep you bound home then you might consider doing extended devotional times in the mourning and evenings and even at noon if you can. The more time you spend meditating on the positive things of God the more control you will have over the emotional and spiritual issues that chronic problems bring.

The final point that needs to be made about how to develop directed thinking is found in the last verse we sited in Philippians. Make a list of things to think about, the list given here is "whatsoever things are true, whatsoever things are honest, whatsoever things are just, whatsoever things are pure, whatsoever things are lovely, whatsoever things are of good report; if there be any virtue, and if there be any praise" Rather than allowing negative thinking, direct yourself to positive thinking. Think about how you can minister to or help others. This process is not easy, it will require a dedication to changing your thoughts but if you will apply yourself to it there is a promise in the Bible that you will be free from the destructive emotional burdens that have added to your problem.

What things from this chapter do you need to implement in your life right now to begin to deal with this issue?

What is the first step that you will take now to start gaining victory?

Please share this with someone you know so that you have accountability to help you make these changes.

Twenty-three

## *Thieves of Hope:*
# *Being Threatened or Bullied*

Bullying. The very word creates fear in our day. It has been around for a long time. For reasons that are foreign to us today, it was seen in the past as something that should be ignored or excused. That may be some of what has contributed to the issue that we face today. The more that bullying is seen as accepted or tolerated by society, the more bullies there will be. For this reason, it is good that this issue has been brought to the forefront of our consciousness. Bullying itself can be defined as a variety of negative acts carried out repeatedly over time. We must refuse the impulse to label every bad or negative act as bullying or the word itself will lose meaning.

Bullying includes any behavior, verbal or non-verbal, that is intended to cause physical, emotional, psychological, or social harm. Such behavior is intended to isolate an individual seen as unacceptable due to physical, intellectual, or even social differences. Acceptance is a very powerful motivator, and, as a result, others who see such actions rarely stand up to the bully because of the fear that they might be the recipient of the bullying actions next. The result is that those who suffer bullying are isolated from their peers, and they experience a severe sense of rejection and damage to their sense of worth as an individual. This can lead to them harming themselves or others in severe cases.

An evil queen threatened to kill the prophet Elijah in 1 Kings 19:2-

4 and it caused him so much fear that he even prayed that he would die. Following this threat, it would also appear that Elijah struggled with a bout of depression. In his case, it is difficult to determine which of these things brought about his desire to die. Depression is a significant issue that many people struggle with. When people threaten us, it can create a significant amount of fear in our hearts. We live in a day when threats seem to be frequent, especially with the advent of social media where they can even be from anonymous sources. This type of bullying and threatening can cause a person to be filled with anxiety and dread. Elijah ran for his life, but the truth is that most bullies are only brave in the shadows. Elijah never was killed, and he ended up doing many more things in his life. Of course, bullying and threats need to be dealt with, but we should not allow intimidation to drive us to the point of suicide. Instead, we should stand up and do what is right so that others can have an example of facing such bullies as well. Jesus faced threats, and even death, for us, and through it, He gave us a way to have the strength to endure. If you would like to learn how to have that strength, continue to read on.

The word in the Bible that best describes bullying is persecution. There are many examples in the Bible that are very clearly incidents of bullying, including the treatment of Jesus Christ and all of the apostles. An example of bullying that I believe we can learn a great amount from takes place in the Old Testament with David before he became the king of Israel. The incident takes place when Saul was king, and David was one of his leaders. The Bible tells us in 1 Samuel 18 that Saul became very envious of David because of the popularity that David had with the people. In verses 8-9 of that chapter it says, "And Saul was very wroth, and the saying displeased him; and he said, They have ascribed unto David ten thousands, and to me they have ascribed but thousands: and what can he have more but the kingdom? And Saul eyed David from that day and forward."

Soon after this, Saul began looking for ways to hurt David. Several times Saul even threw a spear at David, trying to kill him. He tried to hurt him emotionally by driving a wedge between David and his friends, and even forcing David to run away and leading his former friends to hunt him and try to kill him. This is a very severe form of bullying, going far beyond what most people would experience.

Studying David's response can provide so much help because there are several things that we can see in his response that are important.

First, the initial response to bullying is not something that you might want to hear, but it is important for your immediate safety. David got away from Saul when the bullying started. I know that we want to say stand up and fight, and there is a time for that, as we will learn later, but it is not the first thing we should do. The first thing that should be done is to get out of harm's way. Bullying is usually a repeated action. It could be that the first incident is just an isolated situation from which there can be restoration. Everyone has a bad day or responds wrong sometimes. I am not excusing bad behavior, but one incident is not necessarily bullying.

Secondly, we must learn not to overreact to incidents. If we are not careful, we become too reactionary to the point that every cross look is an occasion for retaliation. The Bible says in 1 Samuel 18:14-16, "And David behaved himself wisely in all his ways; and the LORD was with him. Wherefore when Saul saw that he behaved himself very wisely, he was afraid of him." This wise behavior is something that parents should teach their children about how to react when someone does wrong to you. Preparing your children to know how to respond wisely will not only help the immediate problem, but it may also ward off future problems. The wise way in which David conducted himself caused Saul to be afraid to mess with him. Often a bully is simply looking for a reaction. Once they receive the desired reaction, they know that they can push the same button over and over to hurt you. Behaving wisely includes not reacting in such a way that causes them to believe that you are vulnerable.

The third thing to understand in responding properly to bullying is that a person's worth does not come from the approval of others. The bully seeks to isolate his target, making that individual feel alone and worthless. A properly developed sense of worth is not based upon what people think of you, but upon the fact that you have value with God. Do you realize that God loves and accepts you just as you are? The Bible teaches that God's acceptance is not based upon our popularity or our actions, but upon the fact that He created us and desires to have a relationship with us. He loves you so much that He gave Himself to pay the penalty for all the things you have done wrong. He receives you based upon His desire to receive you, not your ability to be perfect. David said in Psalm 73:24, "Thou shalt guide me with thy counsel, and afterward receive me to glory." In the New Testament, Paul says in Ephesians 1:6, "To the praise of the glory of his grace, wherein he hath made us accepted in the beloved." To be made acceptable to God, one only needs to accept God's gift of eternal life through Jesus Christ. Having a full sense of the worth in God is important to effectively deal with the rejection of others.

A fourth thing that must be done if the issue continues is that the person must be reported to the proper authorities. In David's case Saul was the king, so who would you report the king to? In his case, that would be the one who anointed the king. It says in 1 Samuel 19:18, "So David fled, and escaped, and came to Samuel to Ramah, and told him all that Saul had done to him. And he and Samuel went and dwelt in Naioth." Samuel didn't have the authority to remove Saul from being king, but this started a process of God removing Saul's authority and led to the point that Samuel told Saul that God had rejected him from being the king and had chosen to place David over the kingdom.

In your situation, it is not likely that the bully is a king, but it may be that they have some authority over you. If a young person is dealing with a bully, the first person that they should go to is their parents. With help from their parents, they should decide the best course of action that should be taken. It may be early in the process and learning to behave wisely is a lesson that can be learned to solve the problem. If it is further down the road, then going to authorities where the bullying is taking place would be in order. If the authorities will not properly deal with the situation, then the parent might give the child permission to defend themselves. As a rule, this should be avoided as retaliation often tends to go too far. If the authority has set a boundary and the young person doesn't cross it, that may be an acceptable answer. Again, this should be the last case scenario. There can be a case made from scripture that if you are acting under the rule of authority, defending yourself is not wrong. In the Bible, if someone was home at night and a burglar broke in, the homeowner had the legal right to defend themselves in any way necessary. In both the Old and New Testament, God also gives authority of self-defense when appropriate, and after a sufficient attempt to resolve the issue. To be sure, it is generally the one that retaliates that gets caught.

That thought brings us to the fifth thing that must be done: refuse to lower yourself to act like the bully. In the Bible, David had two occasions to retaliate against Saul. Both times, he let Saul know what he could have done, but choose to show grace to Saul even though he didn't deserve it. In 1 Samuel 24:4-5, it says, "And the men of David said unto him, Behold the day of which the LORD said unto thee, Behold, I will deliver thine enemy into thine hand, that thou mayest do to him as it shall seem good unto thee. Then David arose, and cut off the skirt of Saul's robe privily. And it came to pass afterward, that David's heart smote him, because he had cut off Saul's skirt." In some ways, it is good that David felt bad about what he did here even though he was not wrong to do it. The last thing you want to do is become as callous and mean as those who are hurting you. Often, if we are not careful, that is what retaliation can do in our hearts: we become uncaring about the pain that we cause others. Even those who bully should be shown kindness and forgiveness because, without that, we are no different.

For that reason, Jesus says in Matthew 5:44, "But I say unto you, Love your enemies, bless them that curse you, do good to them that hate you, and pray for them which despitefully use you, and persecute you;" God so wants us to have a heart of kindness toward one another that He tells us to do good to people who hurt us and pray for those who persecute us. This goes against what we want to do; we want to retaliate and get revenge, but again, the Bible says in Romans 12:19, "Dearly beloved, avenge not yourselves, but rather give place unto wrath: for it is written, Vengeance is mine; I will repay, saith the Lord." Prayer should be offered for both the victim and the bully, that there would be healing and change. If you are the one that was bullied, then praying for the offender will help to heal the emotional wounds that are in your heart because of it. Vengeance doesn't satisfy like we think it will, but forgiveness heals the hurts that anger never will.

Finally, those who have been bullied should learn that others are in the same situation and need someone to stand up for them. David learned that lesson in 1 Samuel 22:1-2, "David therefore departed thence, and escaped to the cave Adullam: and when his brethren and all his father's house heard it, they went down thither to him. And every one that was in distress, and every one that was in debt, and every one that was discontented, gathered themselves unto him; and he became a captain over them: and there were with him about four hundred men."

David became a defender of the persecuted. He became a helper to others who had been bullied. Helping others in this way will help heal your emotional trauma from bullying. Someone may need you to step up and be on their side. They may need you to be their voice when they are too scared to speak or to be their shield from danger when they are weak. Surviving the bullying yourself, you know what they are going through and you can help them to learn and grow despite the pain they have encountered. This also helps them to realize that they are not alone like the bully is trying to imply, it helps them see that others are on their side and will give them the inner strength to avoid the pain of bullying that some have had to endure when no one would stand up for them.

What things from this chapter do you need to implement in your life right now to begin to deal with this issue?

What is the first step that you will take now to start gaining victory?

Please share this with someone you know so that you have accountability to help you make these changes.

Twenty-four

# *Thieves of Hope:*
# Depression

Ask someone to describe depression or tell you what causes it and you are likely to have a multitude of different answers. Not everyone feels the same way when depressed, nor is the source of their depression the same. For that reason, many who are dealing with depression feel that no one else can really understand what they are going through. This feeling of isolation and uniqueness of problems can hinder us from getting help. If no one understands how I feel or why I feel this way, then no one can help me, or so we might think. In the Bible, we see a number of different illustrations of people dealing with depression and a large number of different words used to describe the feelings. Please consider some of these with me.

After the evil queen Jezebel threatened to kill the prophet Elijah in 1 Kings 19:2-4, he went through a time of depression. "Then Jezebel sent a messenger unto Elijah, saying, So let the gods do to me, and more also, if I make not thy life as the life of one of them by to morrow about this time. And when he saw that, he arose, and went for his life, and came to Beersheba, which belongeth to Judah, and left his servant there. But he himself went a day's journey into the wilderness, and came and sat down under a juniper tree: and he requested for himself that he might die; and said, It is enough; now, O LORD, take away my life; for I am not better than my fathers." Depression is a significant issue that many people struggle with.

The bigger issue that must be addressed is that depression may have many sources. Not everyone who is depressed is so for the same reasons. Consider the following Bible characters that struggled with some level of depression and what the Bible indicates may have been the source of their depression. David's depression seems to have been brought on by rejection seen in abuse and betrayal by Saul as well as Absalom and many other conflicts. Elijah's depression likely came from expectations that were disappointed after a great victory. Jonah's depression was the result of unforgiveness in his heart toward those who had wronged his people. Job's depression was because of grief and chronic sickness. Jeremiah's depression was due to rejection and loneliness. And Ahab's depression was because someone refused to give him what he wanted. Of all these Ahab, of course, is the most sinful in that his was completely based upon not being able to fulfill his lusts. Regardless, I think you can see that many notable people did experience depression and for many different reasons. Maybe one or more of these stand out to you as similar to why you feel depressed.

The Bible doesn't use the word depression, but it does speak of it often. Some of the Bible words that describe depression are given below.

Troubled, bowed down, and mourning as in Psalm 38:6 "I am **troubled**; I am **bowed down** greatly; I go **mourning** all the day long."

Heavy or heaviness as in Proverbs 25:20 "As he that taketh away a garment in cold weather, and as vinegar upon nitre, so is he that singeth songs to an **heavy heart**." Job 9:27 "If I say, I will forget my complaint, I will leave off my **heaviness**, and comfort myself:" Proverbs 12:25 "**Heaviness** in the heart of man maketh it stoop: but a good word maketh it glad."

Sorrow as in Psalm 13:2 "How long shall I take counsel in my soul, having **sorrow in my heart** daily? how long shall mine enemy be exalted over me?" Jeremiah 8:18 "When I would comfort myself against **sorrow, my heart is faint** in me."

Possibly grief as in Jeremiah 45:3 "Thou didst say, Woe is me now! for the LORD hath added **grief** to my **sorrow; I fainted in my**

**sighing**, and I find no rest."

The final term I want to notice is **cast down** this term is used repeatedly in Psalm 42 and 43.

Depression is a devastating and debilitating condition, it robs the child of God from any usefulness for Him, and destroys their effectiveness in dealing with the normal trials of life. All of us are susceptible to falling into this condition, many of those who are great men of faith have been in this state as well. David was a man after God's own heart, yet even he was afflicted by depression at times. The great news from the Bible is that there is a way out of depression. While it is not a place that you have to stay, it is normal to get down, it is a sin to stay there. Psalm 42 and 43 give us a look at depression and the pathway out of it. Notice the darkness of depression as you read through these passages now.

Ps 42:1-11 "As the hart panteth after the water brooks, so panteth my soul after thee, O God. My soul thirsteth for God, for the living God: when shall I come and appear before God? My tears have been my meat day and night, while they continually say unto me, Where is thy God? When I remember these things, I pour out my soul in me: for I had gone with the multitude, I went with them to the house of God, with the voice of joy and praise, with a multitude that kept holyday. Why art thou cast down, O my soul? and why art thou disquieted in me? hope thou in God: for I shall yet praise him for the help of his countenance. O my God, my soul is cast down within me: therefore will I remember thee from the land of Jordan, and of the Hermonites, from the hill Mizar. Deep calleth unto deep at the noise of thy waterspouts: all thy waves and thy billows are gone over me. Yet the LORD will command his lovingkindness in the daytime, and in the night his song shall be with me, and my prayer unto the God of my life. I will say unto God my rock, Why hast thou forgotten me? why go I mourning because of the oppression of the enemy? As with a sword in my bones, mine enemies reproach me; while they say daily unto me, Where is thy God? Why art thou cast down, O my soul? and why art thou disquieted within me? hope thou in God: for I shall yet praise him, who is the health of my countenance, and my God."

Ps 43:1-5 "Judge me, O God, and plead my cause against an ungodly nation: O deliver me from the deceitful and unjust man. For thou art the God of my strength: why dost thou cast me off? why go I mourning because of the oppression of the enemy? O send out thy light and thy truth: let them lead me; let them bring me unto thy holy hill, and to thy tabernacles. Then will I go unto the altar of God, unto God my exceeding joy: yea, upon the harp will I praise thee, O God my God. Why art thou cast down, O my soul? and why art thou disquieted within me? hope in God: for I shall yet praise him, who is the health of my countenance, and my God."

David here uses some very dark metaphors and even some direct statements to express the depression that He is in. Take a special look at verse 9 where He tells us the source of the problem. It says that he goes mourning because of the oppression of the enemy. He doesn't say my enemy, or thy enemy, or an enemy, he says the enemy. While this might be emblematic of saying he was talking about his personal enemy, God doesn't mix works. Jesus used the same phrase to refer to the Devil in Matthew 13:39 when He said, "The enemy that sowed them is the devil; the harvest is the end of the world; and the reapers are the angels." And again in Luke 10:19 where it says, "Behold, I give unto you power to tread on serpents and scorpions, and over all the power of the enemy: and nothing shall by any means hurt you."

Depression is not God's plan for you! God's plan is the peace that passes understanding, He has not given us a spirit of fear, but of power, of love, and a sound mind. Notice that David sees the opposite of his state in verses 5 and verse 11 as he says why art thou cast down, O my soul? And why art thou disquieted in me? Hope in God! David then defines Hope as the opposite of Depression. A depressed person is a person without hope.

David further indicates that the only place to get help is from the Lord. Notice in verse 5 he says that he will praise him for the help of His countenance. Then in verse 11, David says that God is the health of my countenance. In other words, the health of my countenance is found in the help of His countenance. Drugs are not the answer for depression, they only mask the problem, they treat the symptom, not the source. Drugs don't give hope back to the soul, they only trick the brain. David knew that His only hope to escape depression was to get close to God that is why He started the Psalm as he did, As the hart panteth after the water brooks, so panteth my soul after thee, O God. My soul thirsteth for God, for the living God: when shall I come and appear before God?

Now let's take note that this is David, the mighty King of Israel, the conquer of all that he goes to battle with, the man after God's own heart. Many times when we find ourselves in depression we think that we are the only ones who ever felt this way, and there must be something very wrong with us because we are like this, but even David found himself in this state. So, to find yourself in depression is not abnormal, but it is a sign that you are in a spiritual battle. It could be that your depression is because you haven't recognized that battle as such and turned to God for help, or it could be that you have given Satan access to oppress you because of sin.

Remember, whatsoever is not of faith is sin. To be without hope is really to be dwelling in a sinful state. While you might find yourself there a child of God should not stay there. David knows that it is not God's will for a person to stay in depression. But he also is searching his soul to determine where he has fallen into this oppression of the enemy, notice how many times he asks why? A depressed person will often ask themselves, "Why do I feel this way? Why? Why? Why?" The answer is that you allowed your thinking to be co-opted by the oppression of the enemy. As a man thinketh in his heart so is he. What you think will determine how you feel, and how you feel will determine how you act. The key to overcoming depression is to identify where my thinking isn't right, where did I believe Satan's lie, and deviate my thinking from God's word. Once I have identified the error, then I must change my thinking. David gives us five answers on how to do this in this passage.

The first step is to begin to Praise God. Isaiah 61:3 tells us, "To appoint unto them that mourn in Zion, to give unto them beauty for ashes, the oil of joy for mourning, the garment of praise for the spirit of heaviness; that they might be called trees of righteousness, the planting of the LORD, that he might be glorified." Praise is the opposite of depression, the word depression means to sink or to be pushed downward, while praise means to lift up and to exalt. The irony is that lifting God up requires the act of humbling ourselves as well. Depression is the feeling that we are low, humility is though the feeling that He is high. Though you might say these things are similar, the latter comes with a great promise, James 4:10 says, "Humble yourselves in the sight of the Lord, and he shall lift you up." Truly the first step to recovery from depression is to go lower, in humility.

It is not infrequent to find someone who is battling with depression who is also a very prideful person. In reality, they are depressed because they think that they deserve better than what they have received. It is their act of lifting themselves up that has caused them to be pushed down. If instead they would humble themselves and lift Him up, they would be lifted up themselves. I am not saying that everyone who gets depressed does so because of pride, I am saying that humility is necessary for proper praise.

We teach people how to do this in Biblical counseling by having them do a stroke file, they will take a 3x5 card and on the front of it they will write three things in the morning, three things at noon and three things in the evening that they can see to thank God for. David prayed three times a day in this manner. Psalm 55:17 says, "Evening, and morning, and at noon, will I pray, and cry aloud: and he shall hear my voice." Daniel prayed three times a day. According to the book of Daniel, he was so faithful in this that this is how his enemies attacked him. Three times a day you should take time to seek the Lord and praise Him. This will keep His glory before your eyes all the day long. If you are struggling with depression you should begin to keep a stroke file today. On the back we teach people to write the name of their spouse and once each morning, noon, and night write one thing that they can be thankful for about them. It could be things that they do, it could also be things that they don't do. If your spouse isn't strung out on drugs that is a great thing to thank God for.

The next step that David takes is to remember God. This means to look back on your life and purposely remember all the things that God has done for you. When we are depressed, we only see the negative and bad things. It would be good to get a notebook and begin to write down all the good things that you can remember that God did for you. Philippians 4:8 says, "Finally, brethren, whatsoever things are true, whatsoever things are honest, whatsoever things are just, whatsoever things are pure, whatsoever things are lovely, whatsoever things are of good report; if there be any virtue, and if there be any praise, think on these things."

Notice in Psalm 42:6 that David had some special places of remembrance to God. He considered the land of Jordan, this was the promised land, that place of the promises of God. Remember the works of God as He brought His people across the Jordan River and began to give them the place of their inheritance, as David looked around it was a reminder of the fulfillment of the promises of God everywhere that he looked. Maybe there is a special place in your life where you received the promises of God. Consider that place and what God did there for you.

Then David remembered the hermonites. Psalm 133:3 says, "As the dew of Hermon, and as the dew that descended upon the mountains of Zion: for there the LORD commanded the blessing, even life for evermore." The hermonites are the mountain range on the north border of Israel. The hermonites were a place where David had received the commandment of blessing from the Lord. Is there a time in your life that you remember God speaking to you? You should remember that time of God's speaking and think about the times that God has spoken in your life.

David further remembers the Hill Mizar. The hill Mizar is a peek in the mountain range. It is not clear exactly what happened here, but this was a special place for David, and as he recalled what he experienced in this place, it is clear that He remembered the blessing that God gave him there. There are some times of blessing in your life that remembering will bring you up out of depression. There are some mountain top experiences that God has given each of us that will strengthen our hearts.

The next thing that we see David do is to seek his commandments in the day. Consider the following scriptures. Psalm 119:50 "This is my comfort in my affliction: for thy word hath quickened me." Psalm 119:81 "CAPH. My soul fainteth for thy salvation: but I hope in thy word." Psalm 119:114 "Thou art my hiding place and my shield: I hope in thy word." David delighted himself in God's Word and there he found strength and encouragement. Psalm 119:130 tells us, "The entrance of thy words giveth light; it giveth understanding unto the simple." Notice what David did when he had come to a place of depression in 1 Samuel 30:6, "And David was greatly distressed; for the people spake of stoning him, because the soul of all the people was grieved, every man for his sons and for his daughters: but David encouraged himself in the LORD his God." Romans 10:17 tells us, "So then faith cometh by hearing, and hearing by the word of God." To strengthen your faith, listen to the Word. You can get a copy of the Bible and keep it playing in your home, it will strengthen you. It will do a lot more for you than Ellen or Oprah I guarantee. When in times of depression read the Psalms, they are an encouragement to the soul.

David goes on from this and says that to recover from depression you should Sing songs in the night. All through the Bible, we see a strong connection between the spirit and music, Saul, when he was troubled by an evil spirit, had David play on the harp and sing, and the evil spirit would depart. Samuel when seeking the Lord had them play music, David was the sweet Psalmist of Israel, Solomon wrote also Psalms and had a great choir that sang at the temple. Music is an expression of the soul; thus it can not only bring sorrow but joy. A person who is struggling with depression should surround themselves with Godly uplifting music.

The last of the five steps that David took was to spend time in prayer. Philippians 4:6-7 says, "Be careful for nothing; but in every thing by prayer and supplication with thanksgiving let your requests be made known unto God. And the peace of God, which passeth all understanding, shall keep your hearts and minds through Christ Jesus." When in a state of depression many times the last thing that we want to do is pray, when in reality it should be the first thing that we do. Revelation 12:11 tells us, 'And they overcame him by the blood of the Lamb, and by the word of their testimony; and they loved not their lives unto the death." To plead the blood and speak of the testimony of what God has done for us is how we see the enemy being defeated over and over again in the Bible.

This is the place that we find David at the beginning of Psalm 43, He is praying. In Psalm 42 David deals primarily with what the depresses should do, but in Psalm 43 we find out what God does in response to our obedience in these five things. You see Psalm 43 begins with an honest prayer for God to examine Him. He says, "Judge me, O God, and plead my cause against an ungodly nation: O deliver me from the deceitful and unjust man. For thou art the God of my strength: why dost thou cast me off? why go I mourning because of the oppression of the enemy? O send out thy light and thy truth: let them lead me; let them bring me unto thy holy hill, and to thy tabernacles." The word judge here is not a cry for condemnation, but examination and help. It is the thought of one who might inspect an item that is imperfect so that it might be corrected. The last thing that a person who is in depression wants is judgment, but it is the thing that they need, not the judgment of people, but the honest examination of God in their lives. This is accomplished by two means in this passage.

The first way that God examines us is by His light. Light began with God, He said, let there be light and there was light, that is physically, however, the spiritual light began with Him as well, and it is by Him speaking the light into our darkened hearts that we are illuminated. The darkness of depression is a place without the light of God illuminating it, thus He must speak His light into such a place. That doesn't mean that a person who is in depression isn't in the Word, but that God must illuminate His Word in them, the power of the Word of God is His Holy Spirit illumination of it.

Consider the following verses, Psalm 4:6 "There be many that say, Who will shew us any good? LORD, lift thou up the light of thy countenance upon us." Psalm 36:9 "For with thee is the fountain of life: in thy light shall we see light." And Psalm 97:11 "Light is sown for the righteous, and gladness for the upright in heart." Wow, I like that verse. Consider the thought here, light is sown. We think in terms of sowing a seed, but God sows light, that meaning it is planted for a purpose, it is not just floating around aimlessly. Physical light is sown by God to bring forth the fruit of the ground thus making provision for us. Spiritually light has been sown as well, it was sown by Jesus Christ in His death, burial and resurrection. It was also sown in His Word, and it in such a manner has been planted to bring forth more light. Just as things planted rarely brings forth only one of themselves, but much fruit is produced by the planting of one seed, so too much light is produced by the sowing of light. Psalm 112:4 says, "Unto the upright there ariseth light in the darkness: he is gracious, and full of compassion, and righteous." Psalm 119:105 says, "NUN. Thy word is a lamp unto my feet, and a light unto my path." And Psalm 119:130 tells us, "The entrance of thy words giveth light; it giveth understanding unto the simple." God's response to our obedience is to begin to shed His light into the darkness of our depression and illuminate our souls.

The next thing that God uses to judge us is His truth. Psalm 119:151 says, "Thou art near, O LORD; and all thy commandments are truth." Jesus said in John 17:17 "Sanctify them through thy truth: thy word is truth." When God's Word is sent out to our hearts, it reveals what is in error in our hearts. We said before that the reason for depression is that we have believed a lie from the enemy. Only the acceptance of the truth can challenge the lie and correct it. Once we accept that God's Word is truth and begin to ask Him to judge us and correct our error by it, we must commit ourselves to obey whatever He tells us to do. James 1:22-25 says, "But be ye doers of the word, and not hearers only, deceiving your own selves. For if any be a hearer of the word, and not a doer, he is like unto a man beholding his natural face in a glass: For he beholdeth himself, and goeth his way, and straightway forgetteth what manner of man he was. But whoso looketh into the perfect law of liberty, and continueth therein, he being not a forgetful hearer, but a doer of the work, this man shall be blessed in his deed."

The result of yielding ourselves to the examination of God's light and truth is shown to produce results in Psalm 43. Here we find out that they lead us, part of the struggle of addiction is that there is no clear direction for life that is known. Likewise, a depressed person is wandering aimlessly. Life has no meaning or purpose, but God's Word gives a leading and purpose when it is applied to our lives. David goes on to show where God's Word leads us, first He says to God's holy hills, then to God's tabernacles, and then to His altar. There is a natural progression of restoration that is presented here. First, he comes to the holy hills, that is the city of Zion, then he comes to the tabernacles, that is the place of God's presence, and then to the alter, that is the place of my acknowledgment of God.

In everything, there is a progression of accomplishing the goal. The goal in Psalm 42 was close fellowship, here God reveals that to have that close fellowship you first have to get in the right proximity of God's will and reject the lies of the enemy. Then you must come to the place of worshiping Him as He should be worshiped. Once you have been brought to this place you will find what you have been searching for all along. As David says in the last verse of Psalm 43, "Why art thou cast down, O my soul? and why art thou disquieted within me? hope in God: for I shall yet praise him, who is the health of my countenance, and my God." There is health for your countenance and hope for your soul in God if you will obey Him and allow Him to search you and accept His truth.

What things from this chapter do you need to implement in your life right now to begin to deal with this issue?

What is the first step that you will take now to start gaining victory?

Please share this with someone you know so that you have accountability to help you make these changes.

# DO THYSELF NO HARM

Twenty-five

# *Thieves of Hope:*
# Bitterness

Holding on to anger and bitterness can be the source of constant pain. Some who are bitter don't even realize that is what they are dealing with, while others know full well not only that they are bitter but they can tell you every horrible detail of why. While the offense that you have suffered is real, the destruction that you can do to yourself by holding onto bitterness can be far more damaging than you realize. Some know that they are bitter and don't want to continue holding onto it but don't know how to let it go. The good news is that there is an answer, and hope can be restored to you in spite of what you have suffered.

The Bible gives us an illustration of someone who struggled with bitterness and as a result wished they were dead. That is the case of is a man by the name of Jonah. Jonah was bitter toward an entire city because of how they had wronged his people. In Jonah 4:3-7, Jonah told God "O LORD, take, I beseech thee, my life from me; for it is better for me to die than to live."

Several years ago, after being in the ministry for just a short time, I had a foolish conflict with another pastor. The cause of this conflict is unimportant, but the result of this conflict would plague me for most of a year. Finally, God brought me to a place of seeing just how much damage I was doing to myself, both emotionally and spiritually. I praise the Lord that through His word, I was able to forsake the bitterness that had poisoned my soul. This event caused me to look at the bitterness in a new way than I had before. As we explore bitterness for the next few minutes, I will use my example of the struggle to try and bring forth some spiritual truths that will help others caught in this battle to free themselves from the poison of bitterness.

Hebrews 12:15 "Looking diligently lest any man fail of the grace of God; lest any root of bitterness springing up trouble you, and thereby many be defiled;" I grew up in church and a good Christian home. Many times I have heard this verse alluded to and preached in one form or another. Yet I failed to make the connection given in this verse to the source of bitterness in our lives. As you look at this verse, you see the opening warning, "Looking diligently lest any man fail of the grace of God;". Considering this statement, it is without any reservation that I say that the grace of God has never failed, and will never fail. That is not the basis of this statement. The point of the statement is that you and I can fail of the grace of God. We can fail to possess an adequate amount of God's grace to face the trials of life.

Please understand this does not have anything to do with salvation. There are two aspects that we need to consider concerning the grace of God. First, His saving grace. God's grace is able to save all those who call upon Him without fail; yes His grace was, is, and forever will be able to forgive all sin. The other aspect of His grace that is significant is His grace for living. That is to say, the grace that He gives His children to live in this evil world. It is of that latter grace that we are in danger of falling short. James indicates how this happens when he says in James 4:6, "But he giveth more grace. Wherefore he saith, God resisteth the proud, but giveth grace unto the humble." You see two groups here, the humble, to whom God is bestowing grace, and the proud, whom He is resisting.

I think it safe to say that if God is able to bestow more grace upon the humble then that implies that He in a similar fashion resists the proud by withdrawing His grace. Again, not saving grace, but grace for living. In effect, He says, OK, you think that you are something, you think that you can handle it on your own. Well, let's see how you do without my grace to guide you through. God withdraws His grace from our lives in areas of pride. Now, remember the warning of Hebrews, "lest any man fail of the grace of God". When we become lifted up in pride, God withdraws His grace for living from our lives. Then when injustice comes into our lives (it may be real or perceived), with the grace of God removed, we fall into bitterness. We are troubled and are in danger of defiling others.

Let's take a few moments and look at Jonah who I believe was a prime example of the effects of bitterness in the life of a child of God. By chapter four of Jonah, Nineveh has repented, God has forgiven them, and Jonah has rebelled again. Jonah 4:1-3 says, "But it displeased Jonah exceedingly, and he was very angry. And he prayed unto the LORD, and said, I pray thee, O LORD, was not this my saying, when I was yet in my country? Therefore I fled before unto Tarshish: for I knew that thou art a gracious God, and merciful, slow to anger, and of great kindness, and repentest thee of the evil. Therefore now, O LORD, take, I beseech thee, my life from me; for it is better for me to die than to live." Here we find the first of five consequences to bitterness in the life of Jonah. The first consequence is that bitterness causes you to despise the forgiveness of God. Jonah couldn't believe that God would forgive the Ninevites. Some bible doubters wondered if Nineveh even existed. Then in the 1800s, British adventurer Austen Henry Layard rediscovered the lost palace and city across the Tigris River from modern-day Mosul in northern Iraq.

Jonah lived during the height of the Assyrian empire. Based on the tablets excavated in Nineveh, the Assyrians were very brutal, ruthless people. They frequently raided the Northern kingdom where Jonah lived, destroying many villages and towns. The Jews hated the Ninevites. Imagine Jonah's horror when God asked him to take a message to these enemies of goodness. I can't help but picture in my mind this whole city repenting, and Jonah stomping his feet and yelling at God, "I knew this would happen! I knew that if they heard this message, they would all repent and you would forgive them! That's why I didn't want to come in the first place!" Imagine the worst civilization today, and one preacher showing up in the heart of their most wicked city with the message of repent or God is going to destroy you. Would you have so much faith in that message that you would say the same thing as Jonah? We criticize Jonah, yet this was a man who believed God. This also was a man who was proud to be part of God's chosen people. The Jews looked down upon the

Assyrian "dogs"; they were better than these uncivilized heathen. Why would God ask Jonah to take a message of repentance to people who deserved to die? Why not just kill them and be done with it? Oh, how great is the mercy of our God. Yet in his bitter state, Jonah despised the forgiveness that God was giving to Nineveh.

When I experienced the perceived injustice in my life, I began to pray for God to judge the individual that had "wronged" me. I hope that you are more spiritual than I was, but I went so far as to suggest to God what He could do to punish the offender. I look back on this with shame; I was almost like David in his imprecatory Psalms, though operating in the flesh. I did not want God to forgive the offender; I wanted justice for myself. I was proud and wanted God to reinforce that I was right. The biggest problem with this is that when you despise God's forgiveness for someone else, you mar your own forgiveness from God. Matthew 6:15 says, "But if ye forgive not men their trespasses, neither will your Father forgive your trespasses." I place myself under the judgment of God, which means that I have no right to bring my petitions to the throne of God. Psalm 66:18 says, "If I regard iniquity in my heart, the Lord will not hear me". You need to understand that when you are in bitterness, you have cut off your line of communication with God.

It is also important to know that God says in Romans 13 that vengeance belongs to Him alone. As long as you stand in front of the offender ordering God to judge them, God most likely will not. You hinder God from dealing with them because of your pride. What a shame that our insistence on being right can hinder the work of God and bring sin into our own life.

The second consequence of bitterness is found in verses 4-5 of Jonah chapter number four: "Then said the LORD, Doest thou well to be angry? So Jonah went out of the city and sat on the east side of the city, and there made him a booth, and sat under it in the shadow, till he might see what would become of the city." This consequence is that bitterness causes you to develop a singular focus on your enemy to the neglect of your own need. Imagine the city of Nineveh has repented and God has accepted, but Jonah, filled with his sense of justice, goes out of the city, sits on the side of a hill and says, "I am going to sit here until God comes to his senses and kills these people!" I imagine that God may have had more things for Jonah to do, yet he was so focused on his enemy that he could not see anything else. Bitterness causes you to be spiritually blind. I remember during those dark days of my life, asking people who knew this other person, how that other person was doing, but only to find out if God had started the judgment yet. I inwardly longed to hear bad things were happening to them. It is amazing as I have met and dealt with others that are in the gall of bitterness just how singularly focused they are. Their whole life seems to pivot on a singular event or relationship. Often the other party is oblivious to this and lives a normal life, while these pine away in sorrow. Someone once said that bitterness is a pill you swallow hoping someone else will die. Yet, it is you who will suffer, ignoring all the good things of your life, laboring under the false pretense that if God did judge them that it would somehow vindicate you and make you feel better. You have succumbed to a lie.

The third consequence of bitterness is found in the next couple of verses. Jonah 4:6-8 "And the LORD God prepared a gourd, and made it to come up over Jonah, that it might be a shadow over his head, to deliver him from his grief. So Jonah was exceeding glad of the gourd. But God prepared a worm when the morning rose the next day, and it smote the gourd that it withered. And it came to pass, when the sun did arise, that God prepared a vehement east wind; and the sun beat upon the head of Jonah, that he fainted, and wished in himself to die, and said, It is better for me to die than to live." This consequence is evident to everyone but the infected: pettiness. I have yet to meet a bitter person that isn't petty. I have been in church my whole life, but I have only seen one church split that was over doctrine. I was recently told that doctrine divides not among churches. No, it is the color of the carpet, the decorations in the bathroom, the plants in the entryway… the list goes on and on and all boils down to one thing, pettiness. Every preacher could give you many examples of the petty things people have done to others in the church because of bitterness.

Bitter people do things out of spite. Here sits Jonah, the recipient of God's mercy, both spiritually and now physically. He is sheltered in his bitterness by a gourd. How thankful he is for the gourd. And yet as God shows a picture of what bitterness really is to Jonah, a worm that eats at your insides until you die, he gets angry at God again. Bitter people frequently get angry at those who try to help them out of the pit they are in. I am justified to feel this way, they say. If you would have suffered what I did you would feel the same way. Can you hear Jonah crying for the gourd, that petty little thing that was given to help him see his folly? It was unsettling to God to hear him cry over a gourd and at the same time wish death upon hundreds of thousands of people. My pettiness was manifest in the fact that I decided to warn the object of my bitterness in a letter of the impending doom of God upon him. After God showed me my wickedness, I couldn't believe that I would do such a wicked thing. If you and I received the just reward for our sins, God would strike us down right this minute. Yet we have a compassionate, longsuffering God. He was with me, in bringing me through His word to a place of forgiveness.

The fourth consequence is somewhat prophesied in Proverbs 13:12 "Hope deferred maketh the heart sick: but when the desire cometh, it is a tree of life." While the judgment of those you are bitter against will not bring a tree of life into your heart, the deferred hope of their judgment will make your heart sick, and you will eventually sink into depression just as Jonah did in Jonah 4:9, "And God said to Jonah, Doest thou well to be angry for the gourd? And he said, I do well to be angry, even unto death." Maybe you have thought the same thing concerning your bitterness: I do well to be angry until I die. Depression is rarely an organic physical problem or one that is unrelated to emotional issues. It is caused most often by sin. Here Jonah looks in the face of God and says in effect I will not get right. Be careful, there is a line you can cross with God. 1 John 5:16, "If any man see his brother sin a sin which is not unto death, he shall ask, and he shall give him life for them that sin not unto death. There is a sin unto death: I do not say that he shall pray for it." When you come to the place that you tell God you will not get right you are in danger of crossing a deadline with God.

God is very longsuffering and gives us many opportunities to turn but there is a point in which He stops you from harming others. I praise God that He pulled me out of this mess before I came to this point, but I have met many who did not get right. They fell into depression; the world told them it was because they didn't like themselves enough. The truth is that many times it is the opposite: they liked themselves too much. They are many times prideful and do not believe that they deserve the treatment that they are receiving from others and God, thus they fall into depression. You can still be salvaged even if you have gotten this far. It is not yet too late for you to be restored to the truth. The answer is not drugs, though; the answer is the Bible. In just a few minutes we will address a specific answer for you.

The last consequence is unstated, yet I believe is implied and born out by historical facts. Jonah 4:10-11 says, "Then said the LORD, Thou hast had pity on the gourd, for the which thou hast not laboured, neither madest it grow; which came up in a night, and perished in a night: And should not I spare Nineveh, that great city, wherein are more than sixscore thousand persons that cannot discern between their right hand and their left hand; and also much cattle?" Just a little distance from Nineveh is a mosque that claims to be the burial place of Jonah. The scripture is devoid of a further mention of the life of Jonah. The last time we see him is sitting on the side of the hill in bitterness asking God to kill him for the third time. I believe the last consequence of bitterness is death, first spiritual, then physical. The fact that you are reading this is a sign that you still have a chance to get things right, to avoid this final consequence. But how? The answer to that is found where we started just a few pages back.

If the Bible is right, the source of bitterness is a failure of the grace of God, and that failure is caused by God's grace being withdrawn from the proud. It only stands to reason that you must humble yourself to receive the grace of God to cover this sin. James 4:7-9 gives a three-step process to humbling one's self. "Submit yourselves therefore to God. Resist the devil, and he will flee from you. Draw nigh to God, and he will draw nigh to you. Cleanse your hands, ye sinners; and purify your hearts, ye double minded. Be afflicted, and mourn, and weep: let your laughter be turned to mourning, and your joy to heaviness." The first step in the process of humbling yourself is to submit your thinking and feelings to God. Surrender your right to feel anger and bitterness, admit that your thinking has not solved the problem. Your thinking and feelings have magnified the problem and must be surrendered to His thinking and feelings. 2 Corinthians 2:10-11 says, "To whom ye forgive any thing, I forgive also: for if I forgave any thing, to whom I forgave it, for your sakes forgave I it in the person of Christ; Lest Satan should get an advantage of us: for we are not ignorant of his devices." Paul implies here that the only way to forgive anyone is to do so through yielding your thinking and feelings to Christ.

You may have tried to forgive the person in the past; it could be that you even have punished yourself for not being a good enough Christian to stop feeling and thinking the way you do about them. The answer is that you cannot do it through your power. As Paul looked on those who had wronged him (and they were many) he pictured Jesus on the cross. As He was on the cross, He was looking down through time and saw every sin that would be committed, and His choice on the cross was to forgive every one of them, even the ones that would be committed against you. Paul chose to stop going by his thinking and feelings and make a conscious choice to go by Christ's. Forgiveness is a choice, not a feeling. This choice begins with the first step of humbling yourself and submitting your thinking and feelings to God. Submit your wounded heart and spirit, and it will amaze you how quickly He can heal it.

The second step in this humbling process is that of resisting the Devil and drawing nigh to God. The act of resisting is summed up in the act of drawing nigh. You cannot resist the Devil by your own power, but as you draw nigh to God, the Devil must flee. One of my favorite illustrations of the Father's response to us is the prodigal son. I have heard it said it is just as far back to the house as it was when you left. This may be true, but it is not as far back to the Father. The Bible tells us that the Father was watching and when he saw His son a great way off, He ran to meet him. James reinforces this thought when he says to draw nigh to God, and He will draw nigh to you. Every step you take toward God is equal to two. The blessed thing about the story is that the son was in the Father's embrace long before he reached the house; it was the Father that ultimately brought the son back to the house.

The Bible tells us that the Devil is limited in where he can go, and what he can do by the Father. The Devil must keep a certain distance from God, as you draw nigh to Him, the Devil must flee. How do you draw nigh to God? The answer is basic: through prayer, Bible reading, and church attendance. You may say you have been doing those things and it hasn't worked. No, you have been doing those things while filled with pride and being resisted by the Father. You may have been doing the right things, but with the wrong spirit, God was pushing you away. Once you come in a humbled spirit, you will find the Father responds differently to you. Look at these verses: Psalm 34:18 "The LORD is nigh unto them that are of a broken heart; and saveth such as be of a contrite spirit." Psalm 51:17 "The sacrifices of God are a broken spirit: a broken and a contrite heart, O God, thou wilt not despise." Isaiah 57:15 "For thus saith the high and lofty One that inhabiteth eternity, whose name is Holy; I dwell in the high and holy place, with him also that is of a contrite and humble spirit, to revive the spirit of the humble, and to revive the heart of the contrite ones." Humility is precious in the sight of God, He wants to receive you, but you must come on His terms.

The third step in humbling yourself is what is listed in the last of James 4:8-9 "Cleanse your hands, ye sinners; and purify your hearts, ye double minded. Be afflicted, and mourn, and weep: let your laughter be turned to mourning, and your joy to heaviness." To humble yourself and receive the grace of God back on your life, you must confess that you have been in sin. God is not as concerned with the offense as your response to it. You have sinned; you have been in unforgiveness and bitterness. It must be confessed for what it is: SIN. We tend to justify and rename sin to make it sound more acceptable, but God will have none of it. If you want to heal, you must call it what God does, and you must be sorry for it. Not sorry for what it has done to you, but sorry for what you have done to a just, holy, and righteous God.

Let's take a minute to address those who have possibly slipped as far into bitterness as depression. The Bible's answer for you is to begin to look for things to praise God for. Start by setting your expectations in God instead of man as David said in Psalm 62:5, "My soul, wait thou only upon God; for my expectation is from him." Then apply Isaiah 61:3 "To appoint unto them that mourn in Zion, to give unto them beauty for ashes, the oil of joy for mourning, the garment of praise for the spirit of heaviness; that they might be called trees of righteousness, the planting of the LORD, that he might be glorified." Praise to God raises the spirit of man. Begin to make lists of things that you can see and think of to praise God for. Do so audibly, the Devil does not like to hear the praises of God, but the habit of praising God with your mouth will draw you up out of depression.

Back to James, I love verse ten of James 4 which says, "Humble yourselves in the sight of the Lord, and he shall lift you up." He will lift you out of pride, bitterness, depression, you name it, He will lift you up when you follow the Biblical recipe for humility.

One last thing that I wish to address is what happened to me when I finally gave the issue of my bitterness over to God. Suddenly it dawned on me how sinful I had been I remembered the prayers and wishes for God to judge the other individual. I was crushed by this. I began to beg God to forgive them as well, not to judge them. My heart became heavy, and I sought their forgiveness for holding bitterness against them. To this day I pray for them frequently, that God would bless them. When your heart is right, you will not desire the judgment of God upon others; you will desire them to receive the same mercy that you received undeservingly. What joy it is to pray for God to bless others rather than curse them. This must have been how the author felt when he wrote in Psalm 133:1, "Behold, how good and how pleasant it is for brethren to dwell together in unity!" Please, I ask you to heed the warning of the Scriptures as to the destructive nature of bitterness! If you are ensnared by it, follow these Biblical steps to overcome this trap of the Devil. You are not ignorant of his devices. Peace and joy await you when you humble yourself.

God has said that we can destroy the power of anger and bitterness through the act of forgiveness. I know that sounds crazy, but that is exactly what God has done for you. Even though you have broken His law and offended His righteousness, He chose to forgive you by accepting the payment of Jesus Christ for your sin. It says in Ephesians 4:32c, "forgiving one another, even as God for Christ's sake hath forgiven you." Forgiveness toward those who have offended and hurt you is to be done in the same way that God has forgiven you. He chose to accept the payment of Christ on the cross as sufficient for every sin. And if you will accept the payment of Christ as well, then you can have victory over the anger and bitterness that has brought you to this point of wanting to end your life. To find out more, continue to read on.

What things from this chapter do you need to implement in your life right now to begin to deal with this issue?

What is the first step that you will take now to start gaining victory?

Please share this with someone you know so that you have accountability to help you make these changes.

Made in the USA
Columbia, SC
22 October 2024